FAMINE IN ZION

By J.M. Sobczak

Dedication:

For Anna.

Thank you for walking beside me through this project (and every other one)—for the long nights, the painful Sundays, and the quiet ache of spiritual hunger we've often shared. I'm always grateful to sit beside you, even in the hard pews of discontentment, because you remind me that frustration is often a holy longing for truth and light.

I don't always model the spiritual nourishment I write about—not in our home, and not always within myself—but your patience, your strength, and your gentle love have never stopped inspiring me to keep trying.

Never forget that the hunger you feel is sacred. And I am blessed beyond measure to feel it with you.

I love you to all the stars and back.

"Woe to them that are at ease in Zion…"
(Amos 6; 2 Nephi 28)

Table of Contents:

Preface: Let Us Reason Together

This book is written as a faith-promoting critique—one born not out of rebellion, resentment, or disillusionment, but out of reverence for the gospel of Jesus Christ and deep concern for the spiritual well-being of the Saints.

For many months, I have hesitated to write this. I had hoped that perhaps I could keep these thoughts to myself—quietly wrestling with them, praying them away, or simply sharing them with my wife during our Sunday commutes to and from church. For years, I have carried these feelings silently, hoping they would fade. I have pleaded with the Lord to remove this burden from me, to lift the weight of these impressions so I could focus more simply on my work, my writing projects, my calling(s), and my family. But instead of diminishing, they have intensified. With each passing week, I find myself more overwhelmed and heartbroken by what I see, hear, and feel among the Saints—a spiritual emptiness, a hunger we don't yet know how to name.

This book is not an attempt to lecture the Church, correct its leaders, or position myself as any kind of spiritual authority. I sustain the President of the Church of Jesus Christ of Latter-day Saints as the only person on the earth authorized to exercise all priesthood keys. I sustain the First Presidency and the Quorum of the Twelve Apostles as prophets, seers, and revelators. I believe they are called of God and inspired by Him. I likewise sustain the other General Authorities and local leaders of the Church. I do not advocate schism, rebellion, or alternative paths. I reject the spirit of defiance and contention. What I offer here is not a challenge to the Church's structure, but a heartfelt appeal to its very soul.

And yet, I am not naive. I am fully aware that these reflections may be misunderstood or misinterpreted. I know that some members—good, faithful, devoted members—may find these words uncomfortable or even offensive. I understand that this book, though carefully intended, could be misread as pure criticism rather than genuine concern, or as agitation rather than affection. It could cost me friendships, both current and future. It could raise questions about my loyalty. It could even cost me certain callings, limit opportunities, or potentially lead to a membership council. These are hypothetical risks, and I have prayerfully considered them. And still, I feel compelled to write these words.

I do not write these things because I lack love for the Church. I write them precisely because I love it so deeply. I was not raised in this faith. I chose it. I embraced it. And I have remained committed to it—through doubt, through discovery, through joy and disappointment alike. The gospel of Jesus Christ has taken root in my life not as a cultural inheritance but as a personal covenant. Indeed, I have covenanted not only to sacrifice my life in the service of the Lord, but to consecrate it wholly as a sacred offering to his gospel and to his Church.

For over a decade, I have studied the Standard Works with intensity and awe. I have taught seminary, Gospel Doctrine, and Elders Quorum. I've written hundreds of pages of scripture commentary and am currently working on a comprehensive verse-by-verse treatment of the Latter-day Saint canon. My love for scripture is not simply academic—it is existential. And behind all this labor is my love for the members of the Church of Jesus Christ of Latter-day Saints, whose kindness, patience, and compassion brought me into the fold. Without their examples of meekness and love, I would not be here at all.

But love, if it is true, must at times be brutally honest. This book is an attempt to speak hard truths in a spirit of hope. The prophet Amos warned that a day of great famine would come—not a famine of bread or of water, but "of hearing the words of the Lord" (Amos 8:11). In Latter-day Saint tradition, this verse is often understood to refer to the Great Apostasy, the centuries-long period when priesthood authority and divine revelation were absent from the earth following the deaths of Christ's apostles. And indeed, the restoration of the gospel through the prophet Joseph Smith is a fulfillment of Amos's prophecy in one sense—the famine ended when the heavens reopened.

But prophecy is rarely so limited in its reach. Like so many scriptures, this verse may well have layers that stretch beyond a single moment in time. If the Restoration brought a complete end to the famine, then it begs the question—why are so many among us still spiritually starving? Today, we have access to more scripture, more teachings, more programs, and more prophetic messages than at any point in history. And yet, many Latter-day Saints find themselves spiritually malnourished—bored, disoriented, and disconnected from the word of God. The famine that Amos foresaw may not be behind us. It may, in fact, be unfolding again *within* us.

We must understand this famine not as a lack of available scripture or official messages, but as a deepening absence of spiritual appetite and an increased scriptural disengagement. Ours is not a famine of resources—it is a famine of reception and of distribution. In a world saturated with information, Saints may still wander "from sea to sea" (Amos 8:12), seeking something that feels alive, urgent, and divine, and finding only spiritual substitutes.

This famine must not be met with panic, dismissal, or shame. It must be met with purpose. With teachers who feed rather than entertain, with Saints who feast rather than flounder, and with a renewed understanding that the scriptures were meant to be consumed, digested, and become part of our very being.

I hope this work will be received in the spirit in which it was written—as an offering from an earnest fellow Saint who longs not to tear down Zion, but to feed it. The Savior himself declared that one of the defining marks of his true disciples would be their willingness to feed the hungry—"For I was an hungered, and ye gave me meat" (Matthew 25:35). Though He spoke of physical need, the principle extends equally to spiritual hunger. In a time of quiet famine, the call to feed—not merely attend, manage, or maintain—becomes a sacred duty.

This book is written for a wide and varied audience, united by shared proximity to the inner workings of the Church of Jesus Christ of Latter-day Saints.

It is first for those faithful Saints who feel a growing sense of spiritual hunger, though they may not yet know why. They love the gospel. They serve diligently. They have firm testimony. They attend their meetings, fulfill their callings, and seek to raise their families in righteousness. And yet, in quiet moments, they may sense a kind of hollowness. It is a yearning that cannot be satisfied by familiar routines or well-worn platitudes. To these members, I hope to offer language for what may have gone unnamed, and a framework for what has only been dimly felt.

Secondly, for those who *do* know why they are hungry—those who have articulated their concerns, raised their voices, or gently questioned the spiritual atmosphere around them, only to be met with confusion, discomfort, or even disciplinary caution. These individuals may have been told that their feelings reflect a lack of faith or personal righteousness, when in truth their hunger may reflect a *surplus* of spiritual sensitivity. This book seeks to validate their perceptions and honor their courage.

Third, this book is for those who no longer identify as members of the Church—those who have stepped away, quietly or publicly, from the pews they once called home. To you, I do not write with any expectation of return. Nowhere in this work will I attempt to rationalize your decision, minimize your experiences, or offer formulaic reasons for why you "shouldn't have left." I am not here to negotiate your reentry. Rather, I write to extend something that many of you have long needed but rarely received from within the faith—a sincere acknowledgment of what was missing, and perhaps even an apology on behalf of a Church culture that did not always know how to properly feed you. Consider this a no-strings-attached olive branch for the sake of closure, clarity, or healing.

Finally, this book is for those who remain unconvinced that any serious problem exists. There are many faithful Saints, including leaders and authorities, who believe that concerns about spiritual hunger or scriptural disengagement within the Church are exaggerated or unfounded. To such readers, I simply ask for the opportunity to reason with you. What follows is not an emotional outburst, but a carefully studied position grounded in scripture, theological reflection, historical awareness, and pastoral concern. I do not pretend to speak for the Church or its leaders, nor do I ask for agreement on every point. But I do ask for a hearing, and I do so in the spirit of Nephi—"I would that ye should consider that the things which I write are true" (2 Nephi 33:15).

Whatever your relationship to the Church—deeply engaged, quietly unsettled, long departed, or cautiously skeptical—this work is offered with open hands and a full heart. It is not written in bitterness, but in mourning. It is not written to wound, but to awaken. It is not written to divide, but to invite. And most of all, it is written in the hope that the famine which now quietly spreads among us might be recognized, named, and met with the living bread and water that alone can satisfy.

Chapter 1: Feast Upon the Words

From the earliest sacred texts to the modern revelatory canon of the Church of Jesus Christ of Latter-day Saints, the metaphor of spiritual nourishment has served as one of the richest and most enduring symbols for the relationship between God and humankind. This metaphor—where the word of God is likened to food and drink—forms the central axis around which this entire book is structured. As with physical food, which sustains, fortifies, and enlivens the body, so too does the divine word sustain, fortify, and enliven the spirit. This comparison is not incidental or merely poetic. Rather, it reflects a deeply embedded theological claim that the scriptures are not merely instructive, but existentially nourishing—vital to the life of the spirit as bread and water are to the life of the body.

The metaphor of scripture as food did not originate solely within the literary construction of the Standard Works but reflects a far older symbolic tradition in the ancient Near East. Pre-biblical cultures often linked consumption of food, drink, or sacred substance with the acquisition of divine knowledge, transformation, and covenantal participation. In Sumerian and Akkadian mythology, for example, the act of eating is frequently portrayed as a transition into consciousness or civilization. The figure of Enkidu in the *Epic of Gilgamesh* becomes fully human only after partaking of bread and beer, suggesting that nourishment is symbolically aligned with awareness, social integration, and the capacity for reason. Similarly, in Egyptian religious texts such as the *Book of the Dead*, the consumption of divine sustenance is essential for the ka, or spirit, to endure in the afterlife. These foods were signifiers of eternal vitality, divine favor, and enduring spiritual identity. Canaanite and Ugaritic literature, contemporaneous with the earliest layers of Israelite religion, also features scenes of divine feasting, where gods share sacred meals as a ritual expression of authority and continuity. In these traditions, food served not only as a symbol of abundance or blessing but as a medium through which divine-human relationships were enacted and sustained. Early Semitic nomadic cultures similarly treated food—

especially bread, water, and milk—with covenantal overtones, signifying hospitality, alliance, and trust.

Against this broader cultural backdrop, the metaphor of divine nourishment in Israelite scripture emerges as a theological refinement. By reappropriating these ancient symbols within a monotheistic framework, the Hebrew Bible reconfigures the act of physical nourishment into a covenantal, revelatory, and moral encounter with the divine, which would later be expanded upon in Christian and Latter-day Saint scripture alike. In time, this symbolic framework would come to be most powerfully associated with the word of God itself as the ultimate source of spiritual sustenance.

From an ancient standpoint, the phrase "word of God" did not originally refer to written texts. In the Hebrew Bible, *davar YHWH* ("word of the Lord") typically denotes a divine utterance—an event, not an object. The idea of scripture as the word of God is, historically speaking, a later conceptualization which emerged gradually as religious communities began canonizing certain texts as authoritative reflections of divine will. That said, within Latter-day Saint tradition, the scriptures—particularly the Standard Works—are received, revered, and referred to as "the word of God." This does not imply that every verse is dictated verbatim by God, nor that scripture is the sole channel through which God speaks. Rather, it reflects a doctrinal and cultural understanding that these texts are conduits of divine truth, preserved by prophetic stewardship, and authorized by covenantal authority.

For Latter-day Saints, the scriptures function as dynamic instruments of revelation. They are foundational, living, and, notably, incomplete. As affirmed in the ninth Article of Faith, "We believe all that God has revealed, all that He does now reveal, and we believe that He will yet reveal many great and important things pertaining to the Kingdom of God"—implying that scripture is not the endpoint, but part of an ongoing revelatory arc. Thus, even while recognizing that the term "word of God" has evolved over time, Latter-day Saints maintain a sacred relationship with the Standard Works as instruments by which the voice of the Lord can still be heard.

In this light, it becomes important to understand scripture as something living and active, to borrow the language of the New Testament. The epistle to the Hebrews states, "For the word of God is quick, and powerful, and sharper than any two-edged sword, piercing even to the dividing asunder of soul and spirit…" (Hebrews 4:12). The Greek word translated "quick" (*zōn*) means "alive" or "living," suggesting that the word of God is capable of movement, discernment, and effect. This passage does not frame scripture as merely informative, but transformative, suggesting that its true function is not just to be read, but to read us.

A similarly overlooked interpretive layer can be found in 2 Timothy 3:16, which describes scripture as *"theopneustos"*—a word often translated into English as "inspired by God" or "God-breathed." While the term has often been invoked to suggest divine authorship or infallibility, a more careful reading in its Jewish and early Christian context reveals something more nuanced and deeply organic. In Hebrew theology, breath (*ruach*) is the animating life-force of God, the same breath that entered Adam's nostrils in Genesis 2:7, bringing inert dust to life. When scripture is called "God-breathed," it is not just asserting divine origin. It is suggesting that scripture is a vessel through which divine life enters the world. Just as God's breath gave life to humanity, His breath in scripture imparts vitality to His covenant people.

This perspective invites us to consider the Standard Works as conduits through which the Spirit of God may move. This understanding aligns powerfully with the Latter-day Saint view that scripture is part of a broader revelatory process. The scriptures are sacred not because they are complete or perfect, but because they are capable of engaging the reader in a living relationship with the divine. In this way, scripture becomes a place where the breath of God can still be felt, and where the soul can be nourished.

In the Hebrew Bible, we find early expressions of this theme in the Psalms and the writings of the prophets. The Psalmist declares, "How sweet are thy words unto my taste! yea, sweeter than honey to my mouth!" (Psalm 119:103). This poetic exclamation affirms the sensory delight and spiritual refreshment found in communion with divine truth. Similarly, in the prophetic literature, this metaphor takes on a deeper symbolic significance. When the prophet Ezekiel is commanded to eat a scroll, representing the message he must deliver to Israel, he reports that it was "in [his] mouth as honey for sweetness" (Ezekiel 3:3). Here, the act of internalizing God's word becomes literalized in a vision of ingestion, suggesting not merely an intellectual reception but an embodied assimilation of divine will. This theme is reiterated in the Revelation of John, where the seer is likewise commanded to eat a book, which is "sweet as honey" in the mouth but bitter in the belly (Revelation 10:9-10), signifying the dual experience of divine truth—its initial joy and its sobering implications.

In the New Testament, Jesus Christ not only teaches the word of God—he *becomes* the word made flesh (John 1:14), and more strikingly, the food of eternal life. In one of his most provocative teachings, recorded in the Gospel of John, Jesus declares, "Except ye eat the flesh of the Son of man, and drink his blood, ye have no life in you" (John 6:53). This statement, which scandalized many of his followers, is not merely sacramental in reference but speaks to a deeper spiritual reality that Christ himself is the nourishment of the soul. "I am the bread of life," he proclaims, "He that cometh to me shall never hunger; and he that believeth on me shall never thirst" (John 6:35; cf. 3 Nephi 20:8). Similarly, the "living water" imagery, first introduced in Jeremiah and later adopted by Jesus in his conversation with the Samaritan woman, is perhaps one of the most potent iterations of this teaching. "Whosoever drinketh of the water that I shall give him shall never thirst...[it] shall be in him a well of water springing up into everlasting life" (John 4:14; cf. D&C 10:66).

These metaphors, once applied to written revelation, now find their ultimate fulfillment in the person of Jesus Christ, who is both the giver and the content of the word. The transition from word-as-scroll to word-as-flesh forms a theological hinge between Judaism and Christianity, one that the early Saints would continue to reinterpret through the lens of restored scripture.

In the Doctrine and Covenants, the Lord describes his voice as being "spirit and life" (see D&C 84:45; 88:66). The sacramental prayers in both the Book of Mormon and the Doctrine and Covenants echo this theme, inviting partakers to "always remember him" so that they "may always have his Spirit to be with them" (Moroni 4–5; D&C 20:77, 79). In this light, the ordinance of the sacrament becomes a weekly re-ingestion of the covenantal Christ—a ritualized feasting upon his flesh and blood as a memorial act endowed with nourishing spiritual power. This sacred reenactment is poignantly captured in a well-known Latter-day Saint hymn:

> *"As we partake of this bread, bless our thoughts, O Lord, we pray;*
> *And to this our souls be led on the holy Sabbath day.*
> *In the feast of love and peace, may we fully participate,*
> *Ever striving to increase in thy service, good and great."*
> (*God, Our Father, Hear Us Pray*, Hymns of the Church of Jesus Christ of Latter-day Saints, no. 170).

This imagery of ingesting the Savior, the living word of God, is specifically referenced in the Book of Mormon when Nephi exhorts his people to "feast upon the words of Christ" (2 Nephi 32:3). This introduces a level of spiritual engagement that surpasses casual exposure. The word *feast* implies abundance, intentionality, satisfaction, and joy. It stands in contrast to spiritual starvation or malnourishment. To feast is to eat until filled, to savor, to take one's time, and to return again for more. Importantly, Nephi does not suggest that we nibble at the word of Christ when it is convenient, nor that we taste it once and move on. He presents the word of Christ as a continuing banquet—one that is necessary for direction ("it will tell you all things what ye should do") and for vitality.

Latter-day Saints are frequently encouraged to engage in daily scripture study as an act of spiritual sustenance. Prophets and apostles often speak of daily scripture reading as divine instrument that protects and guides us. Elder Dallin H. Oaks once taught, "We do not overstate the point when we say that the scriptures can be a Urim and Thummim to assist each of us to receive personal revelation." President Russell M. Nelson has reiterated similar themes, emphasizing that personal revelation, now considered one of the highest aims of discipleship, can only be cultivated through regular immersion in the word of God. Thus, this metaphor becomes not merely descriptive but prescriptive—one must *eat* daily in order to *live* daily. It is not enough to admire the feast from afar, to acknowledge its beauty, or even to serve it to others. One must partake, be nourished, and be filled.

Similarly, Alma the Younger, in his discourse on faith, uses the image of a seed that must be nourished in order to grow into a tree whose fruit is "sweet above all that is sweet" and "white above all that is white" (Alma 32:42). While the seed represents the word, the act of nourishing it represents the exercise of faith, prayer, and obedience. Thus, this metaphor shifts from passive reception to active cultivation. Spiritual nourishment is not something merely received but something nurtured.

Practically speaking, to feast upon the words of Christ means to engage with scripture in ways that invite transformation rather than mere comprehension. It demands vulnerability before the text—a willingness to be challenged, convicted, and even corrected. It is not enough to search the scriptures for simple affirmation of preexisting beliefs or validation of personal opinions. This may involve serious wrestling, as with Jacob at Peniel (Genesis 32), or questioning and seeking, as with Enos, who "wrestled before God" (Enos 1:2). Feasting is an active engagement with divine presence through words that are alive, layered, and demanding.

The result of such nourishment, if it is true and transformative, is the gradual reformation of the inner life. Just as physical food transforms the body, so too does spiritual nourishment produce visible, tangible, and radical effects upon the inner life of the disciple. To eat, in any context, is to ingest that which becomes part of the self. This process is immediately intimate and irreversible. The food we consume is broken down and ultimately integrated into our bodily structure. It alters us at the cellular level. To apply this to scripture is to affirm that reading, studying, and meditating upon the word of God daily is meant to produce similarly profound effects. It is this transformative experience that distinguishes true gospel/scriptural literacy from casual religious affiliation, and it is the premise upon which the development of spiritual maturity must be built.

Spiritual maturity will manifest in discernible ways—increased compassion, heightened sensitivity to the Spirit, greater patience with others, deeper clarity in moral reasoning, and an expanded capacity for self-sacrifice. In short, the fruit of sustained scripture engagement is Christlike character. As Moroni exhorts, if we "deny [ourselves] of all ungodliness" and love God with all our might, then "is his grace sufficient" to make us holy (Moroni 10:32). This is the ultimate outcome of true spiritual nourishment—not only to survive, but to be sanctified. The word of God, when received in humility and enacted in faith, leads not only to knowledge but to transformation into the divine image.

None of this implies that transformation is automatic. As with physical food, spiritual nourishment can be resisted, rejected, or improperly digested. One may overindulge in doctrinal speculation without grounding in charity, or consume scripture in a spirit of pride rather than humility. The Pharisees knew the scriptures intimately, yet failed to recognize the word made flesh standing right before them. As Jesus warned, "Ye search the scriptures...and they are they which testify of me. And ye will not come to me, that ye might have life" (John 5:39–40). Knowledge of scripture is not the same as submission to Christ. The goal of spiritual nourishment is not to become full of words, but to become filled with the Word.

As disciples mature, their relationship to scripture should evolve. At first, scripture may function as comfort—familiar stories, assurances of love, and moral guidance. But with time, it becomes a call to repentance, to service, and to sacrifice. "Be ye doers of the word, and not hearers only," James exhorts, "deceiving your own selves" (James 1:22). The mark of true nourishment is not just retention, but embodiment. The word becomes flesh again—not in Christ alone, but in the lives of his disciples who carry it forward in word and deed. The invitation remains open to come, to partake, and to be changed, until the image of Christ is written in our countenance and our lives become, in turn, bread for others.

For that transformation to reach its divine potential, a deeper form of nourishment is required. Foundational spiritual principles, though vital, cannot constitute the whole of a disciple's diet. This is precisely the idea Paul alludes to when he writes to the Corinthians—"I have fed you with milk, and not with meat: for hitherto ye were not able to bear it" (1 Corinthians 3:2). The metaphor of *milk* and *meat* functions both descriptively and prescriptively, illustrating the progressive nature of discipleship and the essential need to move beyond the basic principles of the gospel into a deeper, more demanding engagement with it.

In its doctrinal sense, *milk* refers to the elemental truths of the gospel. These include the "first principles and ordinances" as articulated in the fourth Article of Faith—faith in Jesus Christ, repentance, baptism, and the gift of the Holy Ghost. These are the bedrock of salvation and covenantal belonging. Milk, in this metaphor, is gentle, accessible, and nourishing to the young in the faith. This is an essential phase in the journey of discipleship. New believers need doctrinal clarity, emotional reassurance, and spiritual security. As Peter writes, "As newborn babes, desire the sincere milk of the word, that ye may grow thereby" (1 Peter 2:2). Milk, then, is not pejorative. It is a blessing and a necessity in its time.

However, as in physical development, a milk-only diet quickly becomes insufficient. While it sustains for a season, it does not satisfy the needs of a mature body or a mature soul. Paul's lament to the Corinthians is not that they drank milk, but that they *remained* on milk when they should have progressed to meat. Similarly, the epistle to the Hebrews expresses concern that the Saints, though long in the faith, still required foundational teaching when they should be teachers by now—"For when for the time ye ought to be teachers, ye have need that one teach you again…and are become such as have need of milk, and not of strong meat" (Hebrews 5:12). The spiritual implication, that discipleship demands growth, is extremely clear.

In both ancient and modern revelation, *meat* symbolizes the more complex, demanding, and transformative teachings of the gospel—those that require spiritual discernment, moral courage, and deep faith to comprehend and live. In Latter-day Saint theology, this could include doctrines such as exaltation, eternal marriage, foreordination, the plurality of kingdoms, and temple ordinances. These are not "advanced" in the sense of elitist knowledge, but in that they require greater spiritual depth to understand and apply. Joseph Smith taught that "the things of God are of deep import; and time, and experience, and careful and ponderous and solemn thoughts can only find them out" (Letter to the Church, March 1839). Meat, therefore, demands spiritual maturity. It is not quickly swallowed, nor should it be.

This metaphor's biological roots further enhance its doctrinal insight. A milk-only diet in the physical world, while appropriate for infants, becomes life-threatening if prolonged into adolescence or adulthood. The human body, after a time, requires more than milk can provide. Key nutrients must be obtained from more substantive foods. Without them, the body becomes anemic, weak, and unable to sustain higher function. Similarly, the soul that remains dependent on elementary spiritual sustenance risks a kind of spiritual malnutrition. The result may not be apostasy, but it will at least be stagnation.

Additionally, the metaphor of milk implies a kind of spiritual dependence. Milk, especially in the context of antiquity and early Christian metaphor, is something produced by one body for another. It is delivered passively, received instinctively, and mediated by a caregiver. In the scriptures, this metaphor aligns with the role of prophets, pastors, and parents who nourish the flock. While such caretaking is vital, especially for converts, children, or those in crisis, it cannot be the permanent condition of a spiritually mature saint. To linger indefinitely in a milk-only diet is to outsource one's spiritual nourishment to others, refusing the responsibility to seek, wrestle, and grow. The Book of Mormon critiques this dynamic when Nephi laments that people say, "A Bible! A Bible! We have got a Bible, and there cannot be any more Bible" (2 Nephi 29:3). This is the cry of the milk-fed soul content with past revelation or a fixed understanding, reluctant to search for more.

In contrast, *meat* in ancient contexts carried not only nutritional weight but symbolic connotations of self-sufficiency, labor, and preparation. Meat in the ancient world was obtained through sincere effort—hunting, sacrifice, or purchase. It required skill, strength, and sometimes danger. Similarly, spiritual meat is not received effortlessly. It is often the fruit of prolonged study, sacred ordinances, and personal revelation. It comes to those who ask, seek, and knock (Matthew 7:7–8).

In this sense, the transition from milk to meat is not merely about knowledge but about agency. The milk-fed soul relies on others, while the meat-fed soul assumes responsibility. This does not mean independence from the Church or prophetic guidance, but it does mean the abandonment of spiritual passivity. A spiritually mature disciple hungers for righteousness (Matthew 5:6), not just reassurance. They no longer ask only "What must I do to be saved?" but "How may I consecrate more fully?"

Yet, many today resist this transition. A milk-only spiritual diet can be comforting, predictable, and safe. It often demands little critical thought and offers emotional stability. The risk, however, is that such discipleship becomes sentimental rather than covenantal. It may thrive on platitudes but falter in crises. In times of spiritual drought, cultural upheaval, or moral complexity, the milk-fed disciple may find themselves without anchor. They may have testimonies built on borrowed words, but not on personal wrestles with God. A generation raised on spiritual milk must be invited—gently but firmly—to develop the appetite and discipline for meat.

The Lord never withholds sustenance from those who are ready. Indeed, he calls his saints repeatedly to grow up into the "measure of the stature of the fulness of Christ" (Ephesians 4:13). Spiritual maturity is the design of the plan of salvation. Thus, the move from milk to meat is both a divine invitation and a sacred obligation. The early Saints were often chastised for remaining too long in the shadow of spiritual comfort when they were called to be a covenant people of power, holiness, and priesthood. That call remains. "Ye have not come thus far save it were by the word of Christ," Nephi wrote, "with unshaken faith in him, relying wholly upon the merits of him who is mighty to save" (2 Nephi 31:19). In every age, the Lord's people must decide whether they will remain spiritual infants or become "perfect in Christ" (Moroni 10:32).

This invitation to spiritual nourishment finds one of its most sobering counterparts in the prophetic rebuke directed to the church of Laodicea in the third chapter of the Revelation of John. These verses, among the most quoted and yet most misunderstood in all of scripture, constitute both a condemnation and a tender plea. They stand as a critical hinge in the theology of the Book of Revelation, capturing in stark language the consequences of spiritual stagnation and the redemptive promise that awaits those who return to their covenantal hunger. "I know thy works," says the Lord, "that thou art neither cold nor hot: I would thou wert cold or hot. So then because thou art lukewarm, and neither cold nor hot, I will spue thee out of my mouth" (Revelation 3:15–16). This passage is frequently misinterpreted into the binary logic of modern evangelicalism or rigid fundamentalism. It is often said—erroneously—that Christ would prefer outright apostasy to tepid belief, as though divine preference were for rebellion over partial obedience. But this misreading not only distorts the Lord's message, but undermines the deep metaphorical and historical framework upon which the passage depends.

To understand the rebuke to Laodicea, one must first understand Laodicea itself. Located in the Lycus River Valley in Asia Minor, Laodicea was a wealthy and influential city in the first century A.D. It was known for its banking institutions, textile industry, and a renowned medical school. However, one of its great vulnerabilities was its lack of a direct water source. Unlike its neighboring cities—Hierapolis to the north, famed for its hot mineral springs, and Colossae to the southeast, known for its cold, fresh mountain water—Laodicea had no indigenous supply of water suitable for direct consumption or utility. Instead, water had to be piped in from distant sources through aqueducts, and by the time it reached the city, it was often tepid, mineral-laden, and unpleasant—neither useful for healing nor refreshing to drink. This is the context from which Christ's metaphor is formed. It is not a commentary on religious zeal versus apostasy. It is an indictment of spiritual uselessness.

The Lord's invocation of temperature—"cold" or "hot"—is not a value judgment of degree, but of function. The hot springs of Hierapolis were therapeutic, used for healing baths and relaxation. The cold waters of Colossae were potable and invigorating, offering refreshment and life. Both were good. Both had purpose. Both brought benefit to others. What Christ condemns in Laodicea is not lack of intensity, but lack of utility. Lukewarmness, in this context, refers to spiritual stagnation—a kind of religious complacency that offers neither healing nor refreshment, neither balm nor revival. The metaphor is painfully precise—just as Laodicean water caused nausea, so too does a stagnant, self-satisfied religion provoke divine revulsion. The King James translation "spue thee out of my mouth" sanitizes the Greek ἐμέω (emeō), which is more accurately rendered "vomit." The imagery is visceral. Christ is not merely disappointed—he is nauseated to the point of violent sickness.

This reading carries profound implications for Latter-day Saints and Christians more broadly. It challenges any theology of minimalism that would reduce discipleship to outward association, cultural identity, or passive assent. The Laodicean condition is about self-deception. "Thou sayest, I am rich, and increased with goods, and have need of nothing," Christ says, "and knowest not that thou art wretched, and miserable, and poor, and blind, and naked" (Revelation 3:17). This is the heart of the warning—those who are lukewarm believe themselves to be spiritually secure when, in reality, they are destitute. The metaphor is particularly jarring when addressed to a prosperous, established church. It is not the wayward sinner but the self-satisfied saint who receives the sharpest rebuke.

Such a critique is especially poignant within the restored gospel, where covenants are intended to be transformative, not nominal. President Ezra Taft Benson once taught, "When you choose to follow Christ, you choose to be changed" (Ensign, "*Born of God*," Oct. 1985). Lukewarmness is the failure to permit that change. It is not necessarily open rebellion, but habitual inertia. It is attending meetings without engaging the Spirit. It is reading scripture without applying it. It is partaking of the sacrament without remembering Christ. It is religious activity devoid of spiritual power—ritual without repentance, tradition without transformation.

Against this spiritual malaise, Christ offers both a warning and an antidote—"I counsel thee to buy of me gold tried in the fire, that thou mayest be rich; and white raiment, that thou mayest be clothed…and anoint thine eyes with eyesalve, that thou mayest see" (Revelation 3:18). Here, he speaks in the commercial language Laodiceans would have understood—gold, textiles, and healing ointments. But the prescription is redemptive rather than economic. Gold tried in the fire represents faith refined through trials (cf. 1 Peter 1:7). White raiment signifies purity and righteousness, a common motif throughout Revelation (cf. Revelation 7:14) and general temple imagery. And the eyesalve, so fitting for a city known for its medical school, symbolizes the Spirit's power to restore vision—to see oneself as God sees. These are not mere metaphors for private enrichment—they are calls to repentance and covenantal renewal.

Then comes the most disturbing image in the passage—"Behold, I stand at the door, and knock" (Revelation 3:20). This is often cited sentimentally, as though Christ is gently knocking at the door of the sinner's heart. But within the immediate context of Laodicea, the picture is far more harrowing. Christ is not outside the hearts of unbelievers—he is outside his own Church. The church of Laodicea, in its pride, complacency, and self-sufficiency, has locked out the very Lord it professes to follow. He is no longer at the head of the body, but relegated to the periphery, pounding on the door, unheard by the assembly within. The Greek verb κρούω (*krouō*) carries a sense of persistent, even desperate knocking. This is not a casual tap—it is the pounding of a rejected Lord pleading to be let back into the fellowship that bears his name.

For any Latter-day Saint sensitive to the covenantal image of Christ presiding in his Church, this image in Revelation 3:20 should be deeply horrifying. The Savior stands outside the sacrament meeting. Outside the home evening. Outside the scriptures we leave unread. He knocks, not for his own sake, but because his absence renders us, his Church, spiritually empty. "If any man hear my voice, and open the door," he says, "I will come in to him, and will sup with him, and he with me" (Revelation 3:20). The verb *sup*—from the Greek δειπνέω (*deipneō*)—refers specifically to the evening meal, the main feast of the day. This is not a brief visit. It is an invitation to covenantal communion. It is the restoration of table fellowship, the shared meal as a symbol of peace, intimacy, and mutual abiding.

In this final gesture, the metaphor of nourishment returns with breathtaking beauty. Christ, who has just rejected lukewarmness with violent language, now offers companionship and spiritual sustenance. He does not wish merely to be acknowledged. He wishes to dine with his disciples. The entire arc of the Laodicean letter moves from disgust to intimacy, from vomit to supper. This progression reflects the mercy and persistence of Christ's love—that even when he is locked out of his own house, he still knocks, he still speaks, and he still invites.

It is this passage, perhaps more than any other, that has stirred within me a deep commitment to theological labor. If Christ is outside the door, if his voice is misheard, mistranslated, or misapplied, then it falls to the faithful to open the scriptures anew, to reclaim their meaning, and to restore their use. The Laodicean rebuke is not just a critique of individual discipleship. It is a call to ecclesial repentance. It is the reason why some feel compelled to write commentaries, to teach classes, to study doctrine deeply—not out of intellectual vanity, but out of a holy dissatisfaction with lukewarm religion. For what is lukewarmness if not a failure to respond to the living gospel as preserved in scripture?

Thus, the Lord's message to Laodicea becomes a message to every disciple who has ever settled for half-hearted devotion or contented themselves with cultural association over covenantal transformation. Christ does not demand sinless perfection—he demands honest hunger. He seeks not dramatic gestures of allegiance but consistent acts of spiritual participation. To be cold or hot, in his metaphor, is to be *useful*—to bring healing or refreshment, restoration or vitality, and to seek such things for oneself.

The final promise to the Laodiceans encapsulates the full reward of overcoming lukewarmness—"To him that overcometh will I grant to sit with me in my throne, even as I also overcame, and am set down with my Father in his throne" (Revelation 3:21). This is not just restoration anymore, but exaltation. The scope of the Lord's mercy is as vast as his standard is high. But the call is real, and the knocking is indeed urgent.

But what happens when no one opens the door? What becomes of a soul that once supped with Christ but now sits in silence, refusing even to approach the table? If the invitation to nourishment is clear, if the feast is abundant, if the bread of life and living water are freely offered—then what is the condition of the one who walks away from the meal altogether? This final section addresses the most sobering manifestation of the spiritual food metaphor—spiritual starvation. For while the gospel invites us to feast and be filled, it also contains chilling warnings about what occurs when nourishment ceases. The scriptures do not present spiritual health as optional. The soul, like the body, was designed to be sustained, and when it is not, the consequences are terminal.

To fully grasp this concept, one must first understand the physical process of starvation. Modern medical science has long observed that starvation unfolds in distinct physiological stages. Initially, the body responds to the absence of food with acute hunger—an overwhelming biological drive to seek sustenance. In this stage, the mind is fixated on food, and the body rapidly consumes available glucose and fat reserves. But as starvation progresses, something both tragic and counterintuitive occurs—the body, in its desperation, shuts down the hunger mechanism. The brain, deprived of sufficient fuel, suppresses the very signals that would normally compel eating. The person no longer desires food. They may even resist it. The appetite is gone. What once would have saved them now repulses them. This is not a sign of recovery. It is a symptom of terminal decline. The body has moved past hunger and is now in the quiet stages of dying.

This physiological truth presents a disturbing parallel to the condition of the spiritually starving. The scriptures speak repeatedly of hungering and thirsting after righteousness (Matthew 5:6), of seeking, asking, and knocking (Luke 11:9–10). But what if those desires have faded? What if the hunger for truth is gone, the thirst for holiness dried up, and the craving for God extinguished? Is it possible for a soul to become so undernourished, so deprived of regular engagement with the divine word, that it no longer even wants the gospel? The answer, tragically, is yes.

This metaphor is especially apt in our time. In a world saturated with distractions, flooded with counterfeit spiritual "foods," and increasingly disengaged from scriptural study, many Latter-day Saints are no longer hungry—not because they are full, but because they have forgotten what hunger feels like and what real food tastes like. This is the most dangerous stage of spiritual starvation—not rebellion, not doubt, but disinterest. A general apathy toward the word of God is often a terminal symptom of long-term malnourishment. Like the starving body that no longer craves calories, the spiritually starving soul no longer craves revelation, connection, or even testimony.

In such cases, it is common for individuals to speak of "not feeling the Spirit anymore" or of "not getting anything out of Church." These are not superficial complaints. They are warning signs. They suggest a breakdown in spiritual metabolism—the processes by which the soul receives, digests, and responds to divine truth. In the absence of regular spiritual nourishment, even one's memory of past sustenance becomes unreliable. As Alma warned, "If ye neglect the tree, and take no thought for its nourishment…it will wither away" (Alma 32:38). And when it withers, he continues, "ye pluck it up and cast it out." The hunger is gone, and so too is the tree.

A personal testimony, in this context, can function much like emergency rations. It sustains for a time. It can carry someone through a spiritual drought, or keep them alive in a hostile environment. But it cannot replace regular meals. A testimony that is never refreshed by scripture, prayer, or revelation will eventually run out. This is why even returned missionaries—individuals who once bore strong witness, taught daily from the scriptures, and led others to Christ—can later say things like, "I don't know if I ever had a testimony." They are not lying. They are starving.

One cannot help but recall the Lord's haunting words through the prophet Amos—"Behold, the days come…that I will send a famine in the land, not a famine of bread, nor a thirst for water, but of hearing the words of the Lord" (Amos 8:11). What makes this famine especially cruel is that it often unfolds without awareness. People do not recognize their hunger because they have numbed themselves to it. They find temporary satisfaction in cultural belonging, social activities, or ideological causes, but deep within, the soul atrophies. This is why so many who disengage from the Church do so not with a dramatic announcement, but with a quiet drift. They stop reading. They stop praying. They stop hungering. And eventually, they stop believing.

This reality is borne out by empirical data and firsthand accounts. A simple survey of online platforms such as the exmormon subreddit reveals a common theme—before doctrinal concerns, before historical controversies, before moral disagreements—there was disengagement. Scripture study became infrequent or nonexistent. Prayer became mechanical or absent. Church attendance became a chore. The hunger faded, and with it, the ability to recognize truth when it was presented. One could say, spiritually speaking, that the body had lost its appetite and was in the quiet process of shutting down.

It is far easier to say that those who leave the Church simply "wanted to sin," or "never had a real testimony," or "were angry at God." These explanations are clean, simple, and comforting to the faithful. They remove responsibility from the community and place the blame squarely on the individual. But they do not generally align with the actual experiences of those who leave. The vast majority of former members describe not an abrupt severance, but a long erosion. And at the heart of that erosion, more often than not, is a long season of spiritual starvation. This forces a deeply uncomfortable question—When was the last time they were fed? It is a question not of blame, but of compassionate accountability. It is a question that every Bishopric, every teacher, every ministering brother or sister, every parent, and indeed every member must be willing to ask. Did we feed them? Did we offer more than milk? Did we extend invitations to the feast? Or did we assume they were fine because they showed up, smiled, and bore occasional testimony? The ease with which we assign rebellion to the starving may say more about us than it does about them.

Perhaps this is why Jesus, in a moment of sobering intimacy, asked his disciples, "Lovest thou me?" and then followed it not with abstract doctrine, but with a simple imperative—"Feed my sheep" (John 21:15–17). He did not say entertain them, lecture them, or analyze them. He said feed them. Because he knew that if the sheep go unfed, they will wander.

In a physical context, a healthy person does not suddenly die of starvation unless they are cut off from food. So why should we believe that a once-vibrant Latter-day Saint—a missionary, a seminary teacher, a temple worker—could suddenly abandon the gospel unless they were first cut off from spiritual sustenance? Yes, people experience faith crises, encounter disturbing historical information, or suffer deeply personal wounds within the Church. But these are almost always tipping points, not the underlying cause. A well-fed soul may stumble but will rarely fall fatally. The danger lies in the slow withdrawal from nourishment—weeks, months, even years without deep, meaningful contact with the scriptures. Over time, the soul forgets how to digest truth. The very idea of belief becomes foreign. And then comes the moment when, like the starving man offered bread, the gospel no longer appeals.

This is not hopeless. But it is urgent. Because spiritual starvation, like physical starvation, necessitates intervention. The answer is not shaming or arguing. It is feeding. And for those who feel the hunger fading within themselves, the call is not to hide it, but to seek help. If one finds that scripture no longer moves them, that prayer feels empty, that the Spirit is absent—it is not a sign of unworthiness, but a sign of deep need. And the first step is to say, with honesty, "I am hungry."

The second step is harder—to ask whether the Church, in its collective function, is truly feeding its people. This is where the question of Peter returns with force—*Lord, is it I?* Are we offering spiritual meals or just snacks? Are our lessons grounded in the word or padded with opinion and feel-good sentiment? Are our homes centers of nourishment or deserts of silence? Are our meetings feasts or formalities? The answers may be painful, but they are essential. Because if we do not feed the body, the body will die. And if we do not feed the Church, the Church will hemorrhage its members—not because they are wicked, but because they are weak with hunger.

There is hope, of course. Christ is still knocking. The table is still set. The feast is still abundant. The scriptures are still alive. But we must approach them not as decor, not as obligation, but as daily bread. We must reclaim the discipline of daily feasting. We must teach others not just that the scriptures are true, but that they are nourishing. We must demonstrate that the word of God is not just correct—it is delicious.

Spiritual starvation is not merely the absence of scripture, but the absence of Christ. He is the bread of life. We must come. We must eat. And if we have lost our appetite, we must cry out to the One who can restore it. For he promises that even those who are poor, broken, and spiritually malnourished may yet return—"Blessed are they which do hunger and thirst after righteousness: for they shall be filled" (Matthew 5:6). This is not poetic hyperbole. It is the literal promise of the gospel. And it remains open—still—to all who will come.

Chapter 2: Preach My Gospel

My journey toward baptism in the Church of Jesus Christ of Latter-day Saints was deeply intertwined with the scriptures. I was, by all accounts, a difficult investigator. I asked hard questions, resisted easy answers, and required more than superficial assurances. I look back on my interactions with both the missionaries and members of the Church with deep fondness. More than anything else, the missionaries consistently encouraged me to read from the Book of Mormon and to pray about it. During that summer of study, I read through the Book of Mormon twice. I was drawn to its doctrinal depth and spiritual insights, as well as its clear correlation to the Old and New Testaments. My copy of the Book of Mormon quickly became marked with annotations, underlined verses, and handwritten questions.

Despite the sincere efforts of the missionaries, I remained hesitant to commit to baptism. When pressed for an explanation, I would respond honestly that I did not yet know enough to make such a lifelong commitment, and that I felt a need to study further. On one occasion, one of the elders looked at me with a mix of genuine confusion and exasperation and said rather bluntly, "John, you literally know more of our own scriptures than ninety-five percent of the members in this ward." At the time, I didn't believe him. I assumed he was exaggerating—perhaps a well-intended, if slightly desperate, form of missionary persuasion designed to twist my arm in a more charming way. However, the more I continued to study with the missionaries, I encountered a recurring and disconcerting theme of missionaries and members having limited familiarity with the scriptures they were called to teach.

Several missionaries confessed to me that they had read the Book of Mormon in its entirety only shortly before embarking on their missions, while others acknowledged that they had only completed it at the Missionary Training Center (MTC). One elder candidly admitted to me that he had never read the Book of Mormon from beginning to end.

These admissions were not elicited through probing but emerged naturally during our discussions about the gospel. The missionaries often expressed concern that their limited scriptural knowledge might impede their ability to answer my questions effectively.

While I respected their honesty, these revelations were troubling. They highlighted a broader issue within missionary preparation—a lack of comprehensive scriptural literacy. Recognizing this, I began to inquire more intentionally about missionaries' engagement with the scriptures. Questions such as "What is your favorite book of the Old Testament and why?" often revealed a narrow focus on the Book of Mormon, with limited exposure to the other Standard Works.

This pattern is concerning, given that the Book of Mormon, while central to Latter-day Saint theology, comprises only a portion (roughly 20%) of the Standard Works. A holistic understanding of the gospel necessitates familiarity with the Holy Bible, Doctrine and Covenants, and Pearl of Great Price. The scriptures collectively testify of Jesus Christ and provide the doctrinal foundation upon which the Church is built (2 Nephi 25:26).

In one of my very first callings as a ward missionary, I was often called upon to assist in teaching investigators with substantial religious backgrounds, such as lifelong evangelical Christians or Catholic seminary students. The missionaries expressed feeling ill-equipped to address potentially complex theological questions posed by these individuals. I started to suspect that this reliance on ward missionaries for doctrinal discussions demonstrated a deeper systemic issue of institutional neglect regarding scriptural literacy and the formative role of personal study in shaping spiritually competent and doctrinally grounded missionaries.

Some may argue that the primary role of missionaries is to invite others to come unto Christ, relying on the guidance of the Holy Spirit rather than extensive scriptural knowledge. While the influence of the Spirit is paramount in missionary work, it certainly does not negate the responsibility to be well-versed in the doctrines of the gospel. The Lord has emphasized the importance of both spiritual and intellectual preparation—"Seek ye out of the best books words of wisdom; seek learning, even by study and also by faith" (Doctrine and Covenants 88:118).

Moreover, the early leaders of the restored Church exemplified a commitment to scriptural engagement. Joseph Smith declared, "After all that has been said, the greatest and most important duty is to preach the Gospel" (History of the Church 2:478). Under his direction, the Saints were instructed to "go ye into all the world" to share the testimony of the gospel (Doctrine and Covenants 84:62). Brigham Young, too, emphasized the necessity of preaching and teaching the gospel with clarity and conviction, often drawing upon his extensive knowledge of the scriptures to do so. The missionary manual, *Preach My Gospel*, reinforces this principle by encouraging missionaries to study the scriptures daily and to teach the doctrines of the gospel with accuracy and power.

In practice, nearly all MTC classroom lessons—including large-group instruction sessions on core topics such as the Restoration, Plan of Salvation, Atonement, and Book of Mormon—are taught as doctrinal or topical discussions that draw on scriptures for proof-text support. In these classes and in companion-study lesson planning, missionaries are encouraged to use scripture passages (especially from the Book of Mormon) to illustrate gospel principles, but the emphasis is on teaching principles and committing investigators, not on comprehending or even reading contiguous scripture chapters.

Anecdotal reports are mixed on whether MTC training builds strong scriptural literacy. Some missionaries and observers praise the focus on gospel principles. For example, one returned sister missionary featured in the video training series *The District*, which accompanies the Preach my Gospel materials, reflected that after a week of intensive scripture reading at the MTC, she "caught the spirit of missionary work" and began to understand the purpose behind the rules. She attributed this change, at least in part, to "the concentrated daily scripture reading" (Laura Nichols, "*My MTC Experience,*" November 2018). This suggests some find that the MTC's regimen of scripture study, especially in personal or companion study time, can deepen understanding and testimony.

However, other personal accounts note deficiencies. A prominent preparation article warns that too many new missionaries arrive with little scripture knowledge—"I cannot tell you how many missionaries come to the field never having read [the Book of Mormon]! They spend the first 4–12 weeks of their missions just trying to read the book" (Jeremy Goff, Meridian Magazine, "*7 Ways to Come 'Pre-Trained' for Your Mission,*" May 2015). LDS-themed blogs and forums are filled with sprawling comment sections where members—current, former, and inactive—casually confirm troubling trends, such as missionaries bearing testimony of scriptures they've never actually finished reading (e.g., Wheat & Tares, "*New Seminary Graduation Requirements Announced by CES,*" February 2023). These anecdotes reflect a common complaint that the MTC emphasizes teaching *how to teach* rather than ensuring each missionary has internalized basic scripture content beforehand.

The same forum posts and blogs have also voiced concern that the emphasis on "just giving out a scripture reference" can leave both missionaries and investigators with shallow understanding. When missionaries rely on memorized verses or scripted dialogs, they can feel unprepared to answer questions in depth. Some former teachers lament that modern lessons often come from Preach My Gospel rather than the scriptures themselves, and that missionaries are not encouraged to read uninterrupted scripture narratives in the MTC.

One might argue that while the concern of missionaries entering the field without having fully internalized the scriptures is indeed troubling, the responsibility for such preparation ultimately rests on the individual missionary rather than on the institutional structures of the Church or the MTC. Within the Church of Jesus Christ of Latter-day Saints, members frequently reference the parable of the ten virgins (Matthew 25:1–13) as an instructive allegory emphasizing the importance of cultivating one's own testimony and gospel knowledge rather than relying on the spiritual reserves of others. From this perspective, the lack of scriptural preparation among missionaries might be interpreted not as an institutional failure, but as a personal shortcoming—where the primary consequences are borne by the missionary themselves rather than by those they are called to teach.

It could also be noted that the Church has already established preparatory programs such as Seminary, which, in theory, provide four years of scripture-based education prior to missionary service. This reasoning implies that the necessary foundation has been made available and that the responsibility for spiritual and doctrinal readiness lies with the individual. However, such a line of argument requires a few assumptions—for example, that Seminary uniformly achieves its objectives across diverse educational and cultural contexts, and that teenage participants consistently engage with the material in a meaningful way. More critically, this view tends to overlook the potential risks posed to sincere investigators who may encounter missionaries ill-equipped to guide them through the scriptures with clarity and conviction. In practice, the notion of individual missionaries shouldering exclusive responsibility for scriptural fluency does not sufficiently account for the patterns of under-preparedness I have witnessed, nor does it adequately address the systemic factors that contribute to a widespread culture of doctrinal superficiality.

In 2022, I was extended a calling to serve as a seminary instructor for a class composed of students from three wards within my stake. I approached the calling with great enthusiasm and began my preparation immediately. I developed lesson outlines, cross-referenced the assigned *Come, Follow Me* readings with the seminary teacher manual, and took time to learn the names of each student. I also participated in the stake's seminary training meetings. During this time, several members of my ward made offhand comments to me—some lighthearted, others more pointed—about how seminary was a calling they did not envy, and how they, personally, would never want to teach it. At first, I interpreted these remarks charitably, assuming they reflected a general discomfort with teaching or a lack of confidence in one's ability to expound upon the scriptures. Since I did not share those concerns, I took note of the comments but did not dwell on them.

It was not long before I began to understand their underlying sentiment more clearly. On the very first day of class, after brief introductions and an overview of expectations, I mentioned that students would be expected to read from the scriptures at home during the week. This suggestion was met with visible confusion. One student even raised her hand to clarify, asking if I was assigning homework—because, she explained politely, "we've never had homework in seminary before." I clarified that this was not a personal imposition but rather a principle emphasized in the curriculum itself. I further explained that the expectation was not to read every chapter assigned for the week, but to dedicate some meaningful time each day to reading from the relevant sections—even if only a few verses. The goal, I explained, was consistency and spiritual engagement, not volume or completion. Nevertheless, this expectation was met with reluctance, and I quickly realized that, for many of my students, the idea of daily scripture study as part of seminary participation was unfamiliar and even burdensome.

More striking than their surprise at the reading expectations, however, was the pervasive disengagement that characterized the classroom environment from the outset. Many students made little attempt to participate and instead spent most of class time on their phones—playing games, browsing the internet, or watching captioned videos. Despite setting clear expectations regarding phone use at the start of the semester, my co-teacher and I encountered resistance to any attempts at enforcement. Eventually, we opted to move the class from the high council room, where a long table had enabled students to shield their phones from view, to the Relief Society room, where chairs could be arranged in a single row facing forward. This spatial reconfiguration had a noticeable effect—with fewer opportunities to hide distractions, students were more likely to remain attentive. While far from a complete solution, it marked a turning point in classroom management.

In an effort to further enhance participation, my co-teacher and I experimented with various strategies. We leaned into the case study elements of the updated seminary curriculum and emphasized small group discussions. Unfortunately, only a few students—typically a small group of girls—consistently contributed to these discussions, while many of the boys remained silent, often choosing to sit together and disengage. Attempts to involve students by going around the room for individual scripture reading were only marginally effective. Students tended to tune out until it was their turn to read, at which point they briefly focused before withdrawing again. The majority of these efforts failed to yield lasting improvement.

While I had entered the calling with idealism and sincere spiritual intent, my experience as a seminary teacher quickly brought to light a host of structural and cultural challenges. These difficulties reflected a deeper spiritual malaise in which scripture study had been reduced to a perfunctory task, and spiritual instruction was often received with indifference, if not outright apathy. This was particularly disheartening for me as a convert to the faith, someone who had come to love the scriptures profoundly and who viewed the opportunity to teach them as both a privilege and a sacred trust. I had assumed, perhaps naively, that these youth—most of whom were raised in the Church and taught from young ages to value the gospel—would be eager to study the scriptures and deepen their understanding of divine truth.

The experience reminded me of the first time I flew to Salt Lake City, just prior to my baptism into the Church. As I stepped off the plane and into the terminal, I noticed a small table near one of the flight desks with a couple of coffee pots set out. I remember being oddly taken aback, and I stared at those coffee pots for longer than I'd like to admit. Some part of me had apparently expected Salt Lake to resemble a kind of Mormon utopia. That internal reaction was immediately followed by a quiet embarrassment—one of those moments when you're grateful no one can read your thoughts. *Of course* an airport would have coffee pots, just like any other airport. The problem wasn't with the setting—it was with my own misplaced expectation.

And as I came to better understand the reality of these seminary students—just normal, average teenagers—I found myself thinking back to those airport coffee pots, with a mix of familiar discomfort and, perhaps, a little shame.

Over time, I found myself engaged in increasingly deep and, at times, existential conversations with my wife, Anna, regarding the ethical implications of compelling disengaged students to sit through daily scriptural instruction. If I were teaching a secular subject—such as mathematics or English—I might not feel the same weight of concern when students scrolled through their phones, dozed off, or otherwise disengaged from the material. However, I could not ignore the spiritual dissonance that accompanied my role as a facilitator of gospel instruction in a setting where it was clear that the majority of my students did not want to be present. It became increasingly evident to me that, had attendance been left to their own volition, most of these youth would have opted out of seminary altogether. And while there exists a common refrain within Church discourse that youth may one day come to appreciate the spiritual seeds planted in their adolescence, I began to question the moral calculus underlying such logic. Is it ethically justifiable to impose religious instruction in the hope that its value will be retroactively recognized?

In some of the most emotionally intense conversations with Anna—conversations during which I often found myself distraught, even tearful—I voiced a concern that bordered on theological alarm. Drawing on LDS teachings about Satan, I revisited the doctrinal assertion that his plan for humankind involved the removal of agency in favor of compulsory salvation—a system of coerced righteousness that would guarantee behavioral compliance at the cost of individual freedom. With my head in my hands, I posed a disturbing question—in compelling these teenagers to passively endure religious lessons they neither desired nor valued, were we enacting a system more reflective of Satan's plan than of Christ's? It is easy—comforting, even—to dismiss such a question with a reflexive "of course not," and to invoke the presumed goodness of religious education as self-evident. But comfort and truth are not synonymous. Preference is not the measure of moral validity.

As I continued to wrestle with these questions, I came to feel that I was no longer simply teaching gospel doctrine, but rather participating in a system that often prioritized compliance over conversion and obligation over authenticity. The seminary classroom I had envisioned—a space of vibrant inquiry, reverence, and discovery—bore little resemblance to the reality I encountered. Instead, I found myself entangled in a pedagogical structure that, in its form if not its intent, seemed to undermine the very spiritual principles it sought to promote.

In response to the growing sense of futility—and to stave off the encroaching existential disillusionment that accompanied my seminary experience—I arrived at a personal conclusion that if the students were not being spiritually nourished by the standard presentations of gospel principles, then the solution was to engage more widely with the doctrine already available. It was not novelty they needed, but variety. My observation was that the curriculum, as it stood, tended to operate at a surface level. Week after week, vast stretches of scripture, including significant prophetic passages and theologically rich sections, were either reduced to a passing reference or omitted altogether. While it is, of course, unrealistic to expect a four-year program to provide exhaustive coverage of the Standard Works, the issue was not simply one of scope, but of depth and repetition. The consistent reliance on a limited set of "basic principles" risked rendering the voice of the scriptures flat, predictable, and unengaging. The gospel became a kind of echo chamber where students encountered the same dozen doctrinal points in endless rotation, irrespective of textual nuance or scriptural context.

While such an approach might be developmentally appropriate for Primary or introductory Sunday School classes, it seemed inadequate for the seminary setting, which is often framed as a preparatory ground for missionary service and personal discipleship. If these students were expected to one day teach, testify, and answer complex questions about their faith, then surely their exposure to scripture needed to move beyond spiritual platitudes and into the realm of real inquiry and interpretive engagement. To that end, I began constructing supplemental lessons that highlighted less frequently discussed passages that are often passed over in both curriculum and pulpit discourse. My goal was to demonstrate how these texts were not tangential curiosities, but were in fact deeply connected to core doctrines of the Restoration.

To my surprise and cautious encouragement, these lessons sometimes elicited what I can only describe as spiritual "glimmers"—brief moments of recognition, resonance, or awakening in the students. I would see the sudden attentiveness in their posture, the glint of curiosity in their eyes, or the pens quietly reaching for notebooks. Occasionally, these lessons would spark sincere questions, and in rare but meaningful instances, students would remain after class to inquire further about a verse or doctrinal connection I had written on the board. A few parents and ward leaders who sat in on these lessons offered kind remarks, occasionally referring to me as someone with a "deep knowledge" of the scriptures. While I was genuinely humbled by such comments, I also found them unsettling. The lessons I was giving were not particularly advanced or academically rigorous. They were not born of scholarly training, nor were they designed as particularly deep exegetical work. Rather, I was simply teaching what was already present in the Standard Works—doctrinal and prophetic material that, troublingly, had remained unaddressed in the formal spiritual education of these students, and apparently of their parents and leaders. That such modest efforts were perceived as deep dives spoke volumes about seminary instruction.

The scriptures, when taught only as a vehicle for reinforcing familiar gospel slogans, risk losing their transformative power. But when taught with careful attention to detail, intertextuality, and theological context—even at a high-school level—they can come alive. My experience suggested that students are not incapable of engaging with these things. Rather, they have rarely been invited to. And when they are, the results, though modest, are deeply meaningful.

And then my bubble was burst.

One of the stake seminary representatives attended one of my lessons at the start of a new semester. The class itself proceeded as expected—students were moderately engaged, and a couple lingered afterward to ask thoughtful questions and discuss aspects of the material I had presented. However, after the students had left the building, the stake representative sat down with my co-teacher and me for a private discussion. While several topics were covered, the central focus quickly emerged—a word of caution directed specifically at me.

He began by acknowledging that the material I had been teaching was "interesting," but followed with the assertion that it was not "spiritually necessary." He advised, in no uncertain terms, that I needed to "stick to the book." The primary purpose of seminary, he emphasized, was to reinforce gospel principles, not to delve into scriptural passages or complexities, regardless of their doctrinal relevance. The best way to fulfill this purpose, he argued, was to follow the curriculum as outlined in the official Seminary materials. He then asked how much time I typically spent preparing my lessons. I responded honestly that I was investing upwards of 10 hours each week crafting two to three lessons. His response was firm and somewhat dismissive. He told me that this level of preparation was unnecessary and inappropriate, reminding me that seminary was not meant to function as a part-time job.

I left that meeting feeling crushed. I had only just begun to explore the deeper currents of scripture with my students, and I was beginning to see the fruits of that effort—thoughtful questions, moments of genuine curiosity, and signs of spiritual engagement. And yet, here was an institutional representative counseling me to rein it in, to pare back, to conform. I did not want to dismiss his advice outright. After all, he was acting under ecclesiastical authority, even priesthood authority, and I have always tried to heed spiritual counsel. I prayed about it for several days, wrestling with conflicting impressions. I admit, I felt angry at times. Eventually, I concluded that if this gentleman was wrong, the responsibility was his, not mine. I felt compelled to sustain and follow his counsel.

I gradually shifted my approach. My lessons were reoriented toward the specified chapters and themes in the official curriculum. I still sought creative and subtle ways to incorporate context or lesser-known passages, but I carefully framed these within the boundaries of designated "gospel principles" in order to justify their inclusion. I continued to reference surrounding scriptures that were often omitted from the weekly focus, encouraging students to explore these on their own. But inwardly, I felt increasingly constrained, like someone trying to offer living water from a sealed cistern. The vibrancy that had once characterized my preparation began to fade, and I became apathetic.

I shared this shift in spirit with my co-teacher, who had become a friend. He listened empathetically, though I could never quite discern whether he agreed with me or was simply offering space for me to vent. During the following semester, my once richly layered lessons—often illustrated with color-coded diagrams across multiple whiteboards and cross-references to doctrinal patterns—devolved into hastily assembled PowerPoint presentations, many of which I prepared in less than 20 minutes. These were often supplemented with Church-produced videos, which I began to rely on increasingly—not because they cultivated scriptural engagement, but because they filled time and aligned with institutional expectations.

The combination of student disengagement and institutional pressure to prioritize milk over meat left me feeling complicit in a system that— though well-intentioned—seemed indifferent to deeper scriptural inquiry.

I was burned out and increasingly disillusioned. That disillusionment soon began to bleed into other areas of my Church activity and spiritual life, and it remained that way for several months.

I confided in a few of my most trusted friends and my bishop that, for many weeks, my calling was the only thing keeping me active in Church attendance. The very scriptures I once loved teaching became entangled with feelings of resignation, frustration, and sorrow—sorrow over what this might mean for the next generation. If we're not feeding them now, when are they possibly going to be fed? It's hard to find that nourishment happening in youth programs. It doesn't seem to be happening in the MTC. So where?

It is not uncommon for members and leaders of the Church of Jesus Christ of Latter-day Saints to suggest that the formative value of seminary and missionary service lies not necessarily in the immediate internalization of scripture or measurable spiritual outcomes during service, but rather in the long-term developmental effects of these experiences. A frequently articulated position holds that missions, in particular, serve as a catalyst for emotional and spiritual maturation, and that this post-missionary growth will eventually lead to deeper receptivity to gospel principles and a more serious engagement with the scriptures. This argument is often employed in conjunction with endorsements of Brigham Young University, which in many Church circles is still regarded as the educational ideal—the institution par excellence where faith and scholarship converge to shape the next generation of disciples.

Brigham Young University was originally established as Brigham Young Academy in 1875, with a mission explicitly grounded in the integration of secular and spiritual education. Brigham Young, deeply concerned with the rising tide of secularism in higher education and the marginalization of religious instruction, sought to create a learning environment where spiritual development would be prioritized rather than sidelined. In a letter to his son Alfales Young, he wrote that the purpose of the academy was to provide a "good education unmixed with the pernicious atheistic influences that are found in so many of the higher schools of the country." This sentiment was further underscored by Young's oft-quoted assertion that "secular learning [is] the lesser value, and spiritual development, the greater." The academy thus represented not only a strategic educational initiative but a theological and ideological statement about the role of education within the Restoration.

From its inception, the academy was envisioned as a central component of Zion-building—an institution that would cultivate intellectual discipline and spiritual formation in tandem. This dual focus has remained embedded, at least nominally, in BYU's institutional mission, which states that the university exists "to assist individuals in their quest for perfection and eternal life" by fostering a learning environment that is "enlightened by the teachings and example of Jesus Christ" (BYU Mission Statement, November 1981-present). Such a mission, if taken seriously, places spiritual development not as an ancillary outcome but as the end goal of the educational endeavor.

However, for this vision to serve as a meaningful justification for the deferment of scriptural depth during earlier phases of a young person's spiritual education, two assumptions must hold. First, that a significant majority of LDS young adults—particularly returned missionaries—actually attend BYU or one of its affiliated institutions, and second, that BYU continues to embody the vision set forth by its founder.

Regarding the first assumption, data suggest a more modest reality. While returned missionaries make up a sizable percentage of the student body at BYU–Provo—approximately 65% in recent years—and LDS membership is near universal at 99%, broader demographic estimates indicate that only a minority of returned missionaries pursue post-mission education through BYU's system. Based on enrollment patterns at BYU–Provo, BYU–Idaho, BYU–Hawaii, and BYU–Pathway Worldwide, it is estimated that approximately one-third (roughly 33%) of all returned missionaries in a given year enroll in a BYU-affiliated program. As for young adult members who do not serve missions but still attend BYU, the number is almost certainly well below 10%

worldwide, based on overall Church membership and enrollment data from BYU and its affiliated institutions. The remainder attend non-Church institutions, enter the workforce, or pursue other vocational and educational paths. Thus, framing BYU as the institutional remedy for prior spiritual gaps in youth programming assumes a reach and influence that the university simply does not maintain in practice.

The second assumption—that BYU continues to uphold its original spiritual mandate without compromise—has also come under increasing scrutiny. The university has indeed taken deliberate steps to preserve elements of its founding vision. All undergraduates are required to complete 14 credit hours of religious instruction, and an ecclesiastical endorsement is mandated annually to affirm each student's commitment to personal conduct and religious participation. Nevertheless, discussions among students, faculty, and alumni have increasingly drawn attention to a perceived drift from the university's spiritual foundations. Anecdotal reports frequently cite a disconnect between institutional rhetoric and student experience, with some expressing that the spiritual environment at BYU, while visible on the surface, does not always foster deep or consistent engagement with personal discipleship or scriptural literacy.

These concerns are not limited to formal studies or abstract speculation. My own conversations with returned missionaries and BYU alumni have confirmed many of these impressions. Most notably, my wife—a faithful Latter-day Saint and BYU graduate—has expressed that both her mission and her time at BYU were among the most spiritually disorienting periods of her life. While her story is not mine to narrate in detail, I recall asking her, in a moment of candid conversation, when she felt the most spiritually distant or disillusioned in her walk with the Lord. Without hesitation, she responded "on my mission and at BYU." I know she is not alone in that feeling. Her stark response underscores a broader tension that simply cannot be ignored. If the very institutions designed to foster spiritual depth are, for some, sources of confusion, fatigue, or disconnection, then a serious conversation must be had about the extent to which the Restoration's educational aims are being realized—or simply assumed.

The final line of defense for the Church's youth, it seems, is the Institute program—designed for young adults ages 18 to 30, offering weekday instruction in the scriptures, doctrine, and principles of the restored gospel. Although it has one of the lowest participation rates among all Church programs, it is arguably the most consistently thorough and doctrinally rigorous. As a new convert and young single adult in my late twenties, I had the opportunity to attend several Institute classes and found the content markedly more engaging and the instruction notably more nuanced, especially when compared to any other Church class or program I had experienced.

Nevertheless, in recent years, the Church Educational System (CES) has introduced curricula that place greater emphasis on gospel principles and personal application, often at the expense of direct scriptural study. The Elevate Learning Experience (ELE), for example, encourages students to reflect on and apply gospel teachings in their own lives, shifting the focus from traditional content delivery to experiential engagement with doctrinal principles. This approach aligns with broader changes in Church educational materials, such as the *Come, Follow Me* program, which promotes a home-centered, Church-supported model of learning (examined more extensively in Chapter 4).

Once a young adult graduates from or ages out of the Institute program, the only remaining Church-sponsored education settings are the second-hour Sabbath meetings—namely, adult Sunday School, Elders Quorum, and Relief Society. Typically, Elders Quorum and Relief Society focus on strengthening faith through service, ministering, and principle-based gospel discussion tailored to life application, while adult Sunday School places greater emphasis on direct scripture study.

Given that the average life expectancy in the United States is just over 77 years, a U.S. member who attends Institute until age 30 will rely on second-hour adult Sunday School as their sole source of official scripture instruction for more than 60% of their lifetime. With that in mind, one would hope that adult Gospel Doctrine instruction is of the highest quality, especially considering what has been established in this chapter—that throughout childhood, adolescence, and even young adulthood, most members seem to receive little more than a limited rotation of reiterated principles as the core of their scriptural education and engagement.

Following my role as a seminary teacher, I was extended a new calling as Gospel Doctrine teacher for the second-hour adult Sunday School class in my ward. The nearly year-long period I spent teaching Gospel Doctrine stands out as one of the most spiritually fulfilling and intellectually invigorating experiences of my life. Drawing upon the same pedagogical approach I had attempted in my previous seminary calling, I designed each lesson to highlight underexplored or underutilized passages of scripture. These selections were always harmonized with the assigned lesson material and interwoven with broader gospel principles, drawing thematic connections across canonized texts. My intent was simply to elevate the scriptural conversation beyond surface-level engagement.

The response was overwhelmingly positive. Week after week, members of the class offered expressions of appreciation, describing the lessons as spiritually nourishing, thought-provoking, and deeply relevant. Much like the feedback I had occasionally received from parents and leaders during my brief seminary tenure, adult members in Gospel Doctrine often commented that the lessons resembled something closer to "scholarship" or academic discourse. While I was certainly flattered by such comparisons, I must emphasize that my methodology remained rooted almost exclusively in the Standard Works. I rarely drew upon extra-biblical or extraneous material, except in instances where a historical or literary reference enhanced understanding of a specific passage.

What struck me most was not simply the positive reception but the hunger for deeper engagement that seemed to surface in the room. On many Sundays, class would conclude only for a second, informal session to begin, as individuals approached me with further questions, personal insights, or requests for clarification. It was not uncommon for me to remain up to thirty minutes after class, speaking with individuals one by one as they waited to have a conversation about what had been discussed. I was continually humbled by these interactions and often felt that I learned as much from those conversations as class members reported learning from me. Their feedback, their questions, and their spiritual insights sharpened my own understanding and broadened my appreciation for the diversity of gospel experience within a single ward.

On multiple occasions, I received messages for access to my lesson notes or visual outlines. One member shared that an inactive relative had been visiting on a day I taught and remarked afterward that she would consider attending Church more often if lessons were consistently taught with such scriptural coverage. Another individual, who had been in the ward for decades, told me that he and his wife had never felt so spiritually fed in Sunday School as they had over the past few months. These moments were meaningful, not because they affirmed any personal accomplishment on my part, but because they pointed to the great need and desire for meaningful scriptural instruction within the Church's standard curriculum.

What remains most important for me to emphasize is that nothing I taught was new doctrine, nor were my insights the product of esoteric theological training. The content of my lessons remained squarely within the framework of Restoration scripture. What I offered was not complexity for complexity's sake, but thoughtful connections, contextual framing, and the patient uncovering of meaning from texts often skimmed or ignored. I used very simple resources—cross-referencing passages, color-coded outlines, and a chalkboard to visually organize ideas. I am not a particularly skilled public speaker, and my nerves often surface in front of an audience. I found that visual mapping helped me clarify my thoughts, and it allowed students to see the intertextual relationships and theological patterns that might otherwise remain hidden.

This Sunday School calling affirmed for me what I had suspected but feared was idealistic—that there is, indeed, a yearning among Church members for more substantive scriptural instruction. It confirmed that the appetite for gospel "meat" still exists, even if it has been long underserved. Most importantly, it taught me that creating spiritually nourishing lessons is not a question of access to secret knowledge or extraordinary charisma. The people are ready and grateful for a good meal, and the scriptures themselves are fully sufficient.

Anna and I have witnessed this spiritual hunger firsthand in numerous wards across the country, both in places we've lived and places we've visited. In many cases, it has been alarmingly clear that there are pockets—if not entire regions—within the Church of Jesus Christ of Latter-day Saints where scriptural illiteracy is widespread. We have watched with confusion, dismay, and at times heartbreak, as congregations struggled with doctrinal confusion, cultural conflation, and teaching environments marked more by speculation than by substance.

We've sat through sacrament meetings and second-hour classes filled with speculative theology, political commentary, and rhetoric that at times bordered on incoherent or inappropriate—often met not with thoughtful questioning or correction, but with nods of agreement. Talks have increasingly centered on personal anecdotes with only passing reference to Jesus Christ. On occasion, even stake-assigned speakers have exemplified these trends. Reverence has sometimes given way to entertainment and emotional appeal.

There have been Sundays when we've left our meetings in near silence— not out of disinterest, but because we were at a loss for words. I'll never forget the day Anna quietly said, after one particular sacrament meeting, "That felt like a completely different church."

We've never kept a formal record of these experiences, nor would it be appropriate to do so, but we've often joked about how helpful it might have been. Over time, the troubling moments began to blur together—not because they were rare, but because they were so frequent, so diverse, and so spiritually jarring.

In the face of this dissonance, we began to ask hard questions, some of which have yet to be answered.
Why is this happening?
How can such spiritual hunger exist within the restored Church?
Why is the Lord allowing this?
Are the prophets aware?
Are we the only ones seeing this?
Have we entered the Twilight Zone?
But seriously, have we entered the Twilight Zone?
Are other members seeing it too, but reluctant to say anything?
What can we possibly do?

These questions, and others, weighed heavily on us. But amidst the uncertainty, one impression emerged with clarity—the Saints in many places are spiritually malnourished, and most do not seem aware of it.

On one particularly difficult Sunday, Anna and I returned home deflated and emotionally fatigued. We found ourselves exchanging a familiar sort of lamentation—one that had become a recurring feature of our Sabbath afternoons. At one point in the conversation, I remarked with a mixture of sorrow and exasperation, "It feels like we're watching a room full of starving people sitting at a table overflowing with food, and they simply don't know how to eat it." The image captured the tragedy we were witnessing. These were individuals who had access to scripture, to prophetic counsel, and to the full apparatus of the restored gospel—but who had, over time, become so conditioned to the "milk diet" of elementary spiritual messaging that they had forgotten how to spiritually feed themselves.

Over the last few years of personal observation and study, there has been no greater fundamental and egregious departure from true scriptural literacy among many Latter-day Saints than the diminishing focus on the Savior Jesus Christ—on his ministry, his teachings, and his covenantal role in the plan of salvation. Though the name of Christ is frequently invoked in our meetings—in prayers, in the closing lines of testimonies, and in the titles of our talks and lessons—his actual presence in the content and substance of our discourse is disturbingly absent. Week after week, I have observed a pattern in which sacrament talks and second-hour classes rely heavily on anecdotal narratives, emotional self-reflection, and culturally reinforced platitudes, while offering little in the way of direct engagement with the teachings, character, and mission of the Savior. Increasingly, the focus has shifted toward ourselves—our experiences, our feelings, our perceived growth—with only passing reference to Christ as the backdrop to our personal development.

This tendency reveals itself even more clearly in the rhetorical framing of many Church discussions. Rather than exploring Christ himself through the very scriptures which testify of him, we often speak about *speaking about* Christ. We reference his centrality to our theology, affirm that this is "his Church," and repeat well-worn phrases such as "make Christ the center of our lives"—all without actually pausing to study or articulate the content of his message. The result is a kind of performative spirituality in which Christ becomes a symbol of institutional belonging rather than the focal point of doctrinal substance.

To illustrate the absurdity of this trend, I have likened it to joining a book club where, rather than discussing the book itself, the members exclusively discuss how much they enjoy being in the club. Meeting after meeting, the group reflects on how meaningful the club is, how enriching the membership has been, how valuable it is to gather, and how grateful everyone is to have found the club. But the book—the object of shared study and reflection—remains untouched. No one analyzes its chapters, wrestles with its meaning, or reflects deeply on its themes. Were such a club real, it would be rightly dismissed as unserious, and no thoughtful reader would ever return. And yet, a similar phenomenon plays out across countless wards every Sunday, perhaps without exception.

I have frequently observed, in both sacrament and Quorum settings, that once the name of Christ is invoked—particularly if it is followed by direct reference to his teachings—there is often a subtle but unmistakable shift in the room. When either Anna or I have attempted to reorient a conversation back to the Savior, the effect has sometimes been disquieting. In Elder's Quorum, for instance, I have experienced moments where, after offering a comment that draws directly upon Christ's words or gospel principles, the room falls uncomfortably silent. On more than one occasion, rather than engaging with the insight offered, the teacher or facilitator has simply redirected the conversation, steering it back toward anecdotal themes or general discussion about personal effort, family stories, or institutional responsibilities.

Anna, in her participation in Relief Society, has noticed the same pattern—an almost imperceptible boundary that, when crossed by naming Christ too directly or too doctrinally, is perceived as off-topic or even awkward. This has struck us as deeply concerning. If the gospel of Jesus Christ is, in fact, the good news of his life, death, and resurrection—if the Restoration is centered in him and not simply in Church organization—then the consistent marginalization of his voice within our meetings is not a benign oversight, but a spiritual crisis.

At the heart of scriptural literacy is not merely the ability to locate verses or cite references, but to be transformed by the narrative of Christ's ministry, to internalize his teachings, and to reflect them in our theological discourse and lived discipleship. The absence of this focus reflects not only a failure in teaching, but also a systemic failure to model Christ-centered thinking in our ecclesiastical culture. If we cannot speak of Christ freely in the meetings of his Church—if we cannot make him the substance rather than merely the symbol—then we must ask ourselves whether we are preserving the heart of the Restoration or merely its scaffolding.

This concern, though difficult to articulate without appearing negative or critical, deserves careful consideration. It is not a rebuke of the faith of individual members, most of whom are sincere, well-intentioned, and deeply committed to gospel living. Rather, it is a call to realign our discourse and our devotion—to return to the scriptures not merely as a source of inspirational proof-texts, but as the record of Christ's covenantal dealings with humanity. Only then can our worship be worthy of the name we so often invoke but too rarely explore.

It is likely that some readers have approached this chapter with a healthy dose of skepticism, perhaps raising an eyebrow at the emphasis placed on anecdotal evidence or viewing the concerns raised as ultimately inconsequential in the grand, or even eternal, scheme of things. Such a perspective is not uncommon, and those who hold it would find substantial agreement within the framework of mainstream Latter-day Saint discourse. Within that framework, institutional critique, however valid, is often regarded as secondary to more pressing spiritual imperatives of personal righteousness, covenantal fidelity, and long-term spiritual development. The frequently invoked belief that "all will be made right in the end" serves to temper concern, encouraging members to tolerate imperfections, defer critical judgment, and trust that divine compensations will eventually rectify institutional shortcomings. For those who see the Church as guided by prophetic authority and protected by divine oversight, the kinds of institutional critiques explored in this chapter may appear not only unnecessary, but potentially corrosive to faith—spiritually hazardous when placed alongside the eternal perspective.

While such rhetoric may appear humble, faithful, or deferential to divine sovereignty, in practice it too often functions as a theological smokescreen that excuses complacency, discourages reform, and sanctifies spiritual malnourishment. It is not only intellectually unsatisfying but spiritually irresponsible to dismiss concerns about the quality and depth of scriptural engagement in the Church's programs with vague assurances of future compensation.

It is a troubling feature of contemporary Latter-day Saint culture that many members appear not merely tolerant of but indifferent to the fact that generations of young people are raised on a strictly elementary diet of gospel principles. From primary to seminary, and even into post-mission university environments, young Latter-day Saints are exposed to the same repetitive doctrinal themes—faith, repentance, baptism, and the Holy Ghost—while deeper scriptural, theological, and historical complexities are left virtually untouched.

The problem here is not the presence of basic principles, which are indispensable to the faith, but their dominance to the *exclusion* of deeper engagement. A spiritually mature faith must eventually grapple with complexity, contradiction, nuance, and the richness of scriptural texture. Yet what is observable across numerous LDS educational and ecclesiastical contexts is a widespread allergy to theological depth and scriptural breadth. Youth are trained to bear testimony of books they haven't read, of prophets they scarcely understand, and of doctrines they've only heard in distilled form. Missionaries are sent to preach the gospel to the world often before having internalized even a single full volume of scripture. Returned missionaries then become parents, leaders, and teachers, passing on the same underdeveloped scriptural vocabulary they themselves inherited. It is not only a missed opportunity but a self-perpetuating spiritual anemia.

To draw a familiar parallel—"Never trust a skinny chef." The humor of the phrase lies in its intuitive truth that if someone claims to specialize in nourishment but appears never to have partaken of it, something is amiss. Likewise, how can we trust our future seminary teachers, bishops, youth leaders, and missionaries to spiritually nourish others if they have never truly feasted themselves? To merely quote scriptures without having studied them, to teach gospel principles without wrestling with their scriptural origins and contexts, is to offer spiritual calories without substance.

Some defenders of the status quo suggest that this is acceptable because Church members are on a lifelong spiritual journey, and that maturity will come in time. But what if the institutional structures are the very thing inhibiting that maturity? What if the systems in place have so normalized a "milk-only" spiritual diet that entire generations have no appetite for the meat of the word? For if the word of God is indeed "quick and powerful, sharper than a two-edged sword" (Hebrews 4:12), then to dull its edge by reducing it to bland slogans and basic principles is not at all harmless. It creates a vicious cycle.

The underprepared youth eventually becomes the institute instructor, who becomes the gospel doctrine teacher, who becomes the parent guiding yet another generation through an emaciated version of Restoration theology. The problem is not merely that this cycle exists—it is that it appears invisible to many and is even defended as inspired or harmless. There is a disturbing ease with which many faithful members shrug off these realities, invoking faith, agency, or future judgment as reasons not to act.

And herein lies the greatest danger of the argument that institutional critique is spiritually hazardous or eternally inconsequential—it completely shuts the door on accountability. It recasts structural dysfunction as spiritually irrelevant. But if our young people are not engaging with scripture programs meaningfully; if our missionaries are unprepared to answer questions or teach beyond the shallowest gospel slogans; if our educational institutions are no longer nourishing souls as early prophets envisioned—then these are not peripheral issues whatsoever. They strike at the heart of our mission to build Zion and to perfect the Saints.

We cannot outsource responsibility for scriptural depth to the vague workings of divine grace. We must have the courage to say, clearly and without equivocation, that something is deeply wrong when Latter-day Saints can attend seminary, serve a mission, graduate from BYU, and still never have read the Standard Works in full. It is not unfaithful to say this.

It is faithful to the very Restoration that prized the pursuit of truth, even when it disrupted the comfortable.

Chapter 3: The Lesser Portion

In Matthew 7:9–10 (cf. Luke 11:11–12; 3 Nephi 14:9-10), Jesus presents a rhetorical question—"What man is there of you, whom if his son ask bread, will he give him a stone? Or if he ask a fish, will he give him a serpent?" While this passage is typically interpreted within the broader context of divine responsiveness to prayer, it also bears a profound metaphorical implication related to spiritual nourishment. Bread and fish, of course, both staples of ancient Near Eastern diets, function here as symbols of life-sustaining sustenance. By contrast, the stone and the serpent represent lifeless or harmful substitutes—inedible in the case of the stone, and dangerous in the case of the serpent, which carries biblical connotations of deception and evil (cf. Genesis 3; Matthew 23:33). The passage affirms the character of God as one who responds to sincere spiritual hunger with true and nourishing gifts, not with deceptive or empty substitutes.

In a scriptural tradition where food is frequently employed as a metaphor for revelation and divine instruction, this teaching further reinforces the expectation that those who earnestly seek God's word will not be left to feed on metaphorical stones or serpents. In the Latter-day Saint context, where themes of spiritual nourishment are foundational, the passage implicitly critiques environments in which disciples seeking truth may be handed institutional or cultural replacements for genuine doctrinal substance. Thus, the metaphor in this teaching becomes a subtle but potent reminder that God honors spiritual hunger with authentic revelation—not ornamental tradition or corrosive ideology.

In various settings over the years, I've observed sincere expressions of spiritual hunger emerge during Quorum discussions—often hesitantly, but with real vulnerability. Sometimes it comes in the form of a quiet admission—*"It's hard for me to come to Elders Quorum because I just don't feel spiritually fed here."* The language may vary, but the underlying sentiment is remarkably consistent. There is a yearning for deeper instruction, greater nourishment, and more meaningful engagement with the gospel. These moments are rarely confrontational. More often, they are confessions of quiet weariness, offered in good faith. And yet, what tends to follow is not always a conversation, but a redirection. I've heard responses from leaders and facilitators such as, *"Well, I've never felt that way,"* or *"If someone isn't feeling uplifted at church, the problem is with attitude and perspective."*

These responses are representative of what, in certain psychological and spiritual circles, is referred to as mirroring—a dynamic in which any discomfort, concern, or criticism is immediately reflected back onto the individual who voices it. In such frameworks, if a person expresses concern about a group leader, the teaching material, or the emotional climate of the group, the expectation is that they look inward and ask, "What within *me* is projecting this issue?" While introspection has its place in spiritual life, when taken to extremes, this approach can become a tool of deflection. It shifts the point of concern away from structural or doctrinal substance and toward personal guilt or inadequacy. In some high-control or even cultic environments, such thinking is used to systematically dismantle critical thought, suppress dissent, and eliminate the possibility of group accountability. The underlying implication is—if you have a problem with the group, the problem is *you*.

While most members of the Church of Jesus Christ of Latter-day Saints likely do not intend to endorse such an ideology, these kinds of responses reflect a pervasive mindset—often unconscious—found among many well-meaning Saints. The impulse to redirect discomfort back onto the individual is often seen as an expression of faith or loyalty. But such responses, while perhaps rooted in good intent, can render certain concerns unutterable. They close the door to necessary conversations and disincentivize reflection on systemic or cultural deficiencies within our worship environments. More importantly, they can invalidate genuine spiritual hunger. Many members simply do not know how to articulate their discontent, let alone examine it, because we have not cultivated a culture that teaches people how to safely or constructively engage in such dialogue.

In one instance, I listened to a sister give a sacrament meeting talk in which she commented on the oft-heard refrain, "I'm not getting anything out of church." She strongly rebuked the sentiment and countered with, "Whoever said you needed to get anything out of church? Church isn't about you—it's about the people around you." She went on to suggest that even if one feels no desire to attend, they should come anyway, because their smile or presence might be what convinces someone else to return the following week. While such statements may be rhetorically stirring, they are, at their core, theologically and pastorally problematic. They reduce religious observance to an act of performative duty and burden individuals with the emotional weight of others' spiritual outcomes. Over time, this can create an environment where attendance is driven more by guilt than by grace, more by obligation than by nourishment. It becomes, in effect, a pressure cooker for resentment and quiet disengagement.

If someone were to tell me they are not getting anything out of church, my instinct is not to question their commitment, attitude, or faith. My first questions would be: What is being offered there? Is there spiritual substance present? Is the doctrine of Christ being taught in clarity and depth? Are the scriptures being meaningfully engaged? Or is the content closer to a steady stream of empty calories, lightly dusted with gospel language but lacking the theological nutrition that the soul requires?

Part of what makes scriptural illiteracy particularly insidious is that it rarely presents as a crisis. On the surface, everything seems intact— meetings are held, callings are filled, talks are given, activities proceed. A ward may even appear highly functional by conventional metrics— warmth, friendliness, activity rates. But beneath this institutional momentum, something may be spiritually hollow. Elder Donald L. Hallstrom once observed that "It is possible to be active in the Church and less active in the gospel" ("*Converted to His Gospel through His Church*," April 2012). That distinction between activity and discipleship is rarely examined, yet it explains why some of the most earnest and faithful members quietly slip away. They were not spiritually lazy. They were spiritually hungry. And they were given a stone.

It is important to acknowledge that the suggestion of a widespread deficiency within Church culture—particularly the idea that certain wards or stakes may be failing to adequately spiritually nourish their members—can be deeply uncomfortable, even offensive, to some. This discomfort is not without reason. For many, the instinct to defend one's religious community arises from a genuine sense of loyalty, gratitude, and reverence for the good it has done. There is virtue in wanting to protect one's community from criticism, especially when that criticism appears to challenge its sincerity or integrity. Such sensitivities must be respected and engaged with care.

Therefore, for the rhetorical and analytical purposes of this chapter, I invite the reader to step into a slightly more distanced and reflective frame—one that temporarily suspends judgment or defensiveness and instead allows for a kind of thought experiment grounded in theological and cultural inquiry. Rather than offering a litany of grievances or assigning blame to specific individuals or groups, the question posed here is both hypothetical and diagnostic in nature—*If* scriptural illiteracy were to become a widespread problem within the Church *what would we expect to observe?* What patterns of behavior, speech, or spiritual sentiment might emerge as outward symptoms of a deeper inward deficiency?

If, upon reading what follows, one finds no correlation between the proposed observations and their own experiences, then no harm is done. At worst, one has been invited to consider a range of warning signs, blind spots, and red flags, and will be better equipped to recognize them if they should arise in the future. However, if the reader does find resonance—if the descriptions and reflections that follow strike a little too close to home or confirm long-held impressions that previously lacked vocabulary—then perhaps this exercise will serve as an invitation to engage these realities with sincere, critical thought. The goal is not to condemn, but to illuminate. For those who feel the dissonance, this chapter offers a framework for honest confrontation and faithful response—a beginning point for addressing systemic spiritual malnourishment with both reverence for the Restoration and a firm commitment to its continuing vitality.

The following material presents a series of thematically grouped and logically ordered categories of observable outcomes that may reasonably be expected in contexts where scriptural illiteracy is present. To further illuminate the progressive and often imperceptible nature of this decline, each section is accompanied by a corresponding metaphor drawn from the stages of starvation. These parallels serve as a symbolic framework for understanding how spiritual vitality can erode when scripture ceases to function as the living center of discipleship.

Stage 1 – Foundational Weaknesses in Gospel Learning
Starvation Stage: Nutrient Deficiency / Initial Malnutrition

Reduction in Doctrinal Depth

If scriptural illiteracy were to become widespread within the Church, one of the earliest and most consistent outcomes would be a reduction in doctrinal depth. This would manifest as a gradual flattening of teaching, testimony, and discourse. Lessons and sacrament talks would increasingly rely on familiar clichés, generalized encouragements, or culturally comfortable phrases rather than meaningful engagement with revealed doctrine. Scriptural exposition would give way to anecdotal storytelling, while theological reflection would be replaced by personal opinion.

In such an environment, the effects of prophetic teaching would also be dulled. Prophets and apostles often teach through layered scriptural allusions, drawing on shared canonical memory. In wards or stakes where scriptural literacy has declined, these allusions would fall flat. Talks rich in interpretive depth would be received as little more than motivational speeches, and the revelatory thread lost. Members would learn to respond to the emotional tone of a message without recognizing its doctrinal core. In time, the Church could become rich in sentiment but

51

impoverished in real theology. The gospel, in such settings, would cease to be a revealed structure of truth and instead become a series of impressions loosely tied to tradition.

This decline would be especially visible in relation to the Book of Mormon—the most widely circulated and, ostensibly, most studied volume of scripture within the Church. What would likely tend to remain are the well-worn phrases and narrative touchstones frequently cited in primary, seminary, and General Conference: "I will go and do," "Adam fell that men might be," "If ye shall ask with a sincere heart," and so on. Likewise, familiar stories—Nephi retrieving the plates, Lehi's vision, the martyrdom of Abinadi, Captain Moroni's banner, the stripling warriors— would dominate spiritual discourse. While not inappropriate, their repetition without deeper doctrinal exposition would contribute to surface-level engagement.

What would subsequently fade are the doctrine's that define the Book of Mormon's covenantal urgency. For example: Mosiah's denunciation of monarchy (Mosiah 29), Alma's rebuke of wealth inequality (Alma 4), the blueprint for a Zion society (4 Nephi), and the severe warnings to the modern Gentile Church (3 Nephi 16; Ether 2–3). These are central to the Book's prophetic voice. In scripturally shallow environments, they would often be left untouched, reducing the Book of Mormon to a treasury of stories rather than the covenantal record and warning voice it claims to be.

Collapse of Internal Scriptural Canon Cross-Talk

If scriptural illiteracy were to become widespread within the Church, one of the more subtle but damaging outcomes would be the collapse of internal canon cross-talk. In Latter-day Saint tradition, scripture is a tapestry of interwoven revelation—each part interpreting, reinforcing, recontextualizing, fulfilling, and unifying the others. But where scriptural engagement is minimal, this intertextuality will disappear, and the scriptures would begin to function more like disconnected documents than a coherent canon. Ironically, this would align the church more with mainstream academic and secular views of scripture.

In scripturally shallow environments, members would recognize familiar verses but lack the context or cross-canonical awareness to connect them. Over time, the Restoration's scriptural canon would cease to interpret itself and would instead be shaped by personal opinion, cultural trends, or isolated proof-texting.

<u>Over-Reliance on Leadership Authority</u>

If scriptural illiteracy were to become widespread within the Church, there would be an over-reliance on leadership authority at the expense of direct engagement with scripture. While reverence for prophetic leadership is foundational in Latter-day Saint theology, it becomes problematic when leadership voices functionally replace the scriptural canon as the primary source of doctrinal understanding.

In such environments, members would often default to familiar leadership statements as their core doctrinal references—not because these are more inspired, but because they are more accessible, more frequently cited, and culturally reinforced. Scripture, especially when it is complex, symbolic, or unfamiliar, would increasingly be bypassed in favor of concise quotations from general authorities. The implicit message would essentially become—*Let the Brethren tell us what the scriptures mean,* or worse, *Let them replace the scriptures altogether.*

This shift would foster a model of gospel learning that is derivative and spiritually dependent. Rather than cultivating doctrinal discernment through scripture and the Spirit, members would begin to defer their understanding—and even their conscience—to perceived institutional consensus. In place of spiritually confident, scripturally literate disciples, we would end up with Saints who see themselves not as students of the word, but as passive recipients of filtered instruction.

Overuse of General Conference as a Substitute for Canon

If scriptural illiteracy were to become widespread within the Church, there would be an overreliance on General Conference talks as a functional substitute for scripture. Conference talks are generally more emotionally resonant and linguistically modern than scripture, making them a natural default for talks, lessons, and even personal study. However, when these addresses are referenced independently of their scriptural foundation, the risk of theological distortion will increase. Prophetic interpretation may eventually be mistaken for original doctrine, and counsel given in specific historical contexts may be viewed as universal or timeless revelation. When scripture is marginalized, members may not only misapply prophetic counsel but also miss the rich web of scriptural allusion embedded within it.

Imbalance Between Policy and Principle

If scriptural illiteracy were to become widespread within the Church, there would be an increasing imbalance between policy and principle. In such environments, Church policies—outlined in handbooks, procedures, and cultural expectations—would gradually become the default lens through which righteousness is interpreted. While policy is vital for order and consistency, it is not meant to function independently of the doctrinal principles that give it meaning. When scripture no longer informs the spiritual life of the membership, policy often rises to prominence.

This imbalance is largely structural. Policy is easier to reference. It is clear, procedural, and typically requires no interpretive wrestling. It provides certainty through lists of do's and don'ts that fill the vacuum left by underdeveloped scriptural understanding. In this context, members may ask, "Is it allowed?" or "What does the handbook say?" rather than, "What does the Lord teach in scripture?" or "How does this align with grace, agency, or discipleship?"

Over time, members would start to lack the tools to apply policy *wisely*. The Word of Wisdom becomes a health checklist, not a covenant discipline. Modesty becomes hemline enforcement, not a principle of holiness and embodiment. Over time, this fosters a culture of regulation over transformation. Worthiness becomes behavioral compliance. Questions feel unsafe. Leaders prioritize enforcement over discernment. Policy becomes the measure of righteousness.

This is rarely the result of authoritarian intent. More often, it reflects a desire for safety and orthodoxy in the absence of scriptural fluency. But policy cannot build Zion. The Restoration is not a legal code—it is a covenantal call to live by revealed principles, guided by scripture and personal revelation. In a scripturally literate Church, members will still honor policy, but with discernment, compassion, and purpose. Without that foundation, Church life risks becoming precise in form and hollow in substance.

Overreliance on Institutionalized Faith

If scriptural illiteracy were to become widespread within the Church, one likely consequence would be an overreliance on institutionalized faith. This overreliance would produce a model in which Church participation is mistaken for spiritual transformation. In such environments, outward engagement with Church structures—attendance, callings, behavioral norms—would begin to substitute for discipleship, doctrinal understanding, and personal conversion. Over time, checklist spirituality would replace the deeper, nourishing dimensions of gospel living, including a relationship with Jesus Christ.

Elder Donald L. Hallstrom's distinction between "active in the Church" and "active in the gospel" is critical. The Church should facilitate discipleship, but it is not a substitute for it. Without scriptural literacy, members may feel spiritually "active" simply because they are punctual, busy, or compliant, all the while remaining inwardly malnourished.

This deficiency would be reflected in language and teaching. Testimonies would focus on knowing "the Church is true," while references to Christ or scripture are minimal. Lessons would center on following counsel and fulfilling roles, not studying doctrine or exploring the Standard Works. The Church would be seen not only as the body of Christ, but as the source of Christ—bypassing the very scriptures that testify of him.

Stage 2 – Cracks in Doctrinal Application
Starvation Stage: Metabolic Deterioration / Functional Breakdown

Weak Gospel Teaching

If scriptural illiteracy were to become widespread within the Church, there would be a decline in the quality of gospel teaching across age groups and settings. When scripture is not a regular part of members' spiritual lives, those called to teach may lack both the tools and the foundation needed to anchor their lessons in revealed truth. In such conditions, official Church classes would shift toward anecdotal teaching—relying on personal stories and emotional experiences rather than structured engagement with scripture. Lessons would center on broad moral platitudes or vague spiritual impressions, with scripture present in name but not in substance.

This trend would lead to "discussion-only" formats, where underprepared teachers default to open-ended questions with minimal doctrinal framing. While participatory learning is valuable, when detached from scriptural exposition, it risks reinforcing opinion rather than exploring truth. Teachers may avoid citing scripture altogether, unsure of their authority to interpret it, further weakening classroom dynamic. The effect would be especially acute in youth programs. Activities would prioritize fun, service, or social bonding, while doctrinal instruction would fade to the margins. Emotional loyalty to Church culture cannot substitute for rootedness in truth. Without opportunities to wrestle with scripture and explore real questions, youth will enter adulthood ill-equipped for spiritual complexity.

Priesthood and Relief Society Lessons Feel Like Self-Help Discourse

If scriptural illiteracy were to become widespread within the Church, Elders Quorum and Relief Society gospel instruction would transform into formats resembling motivational presentations or group therapy sessions. Lessons would focus on broad virtues like "hope," "resilience," or "kindness," framed through personal stories or inspirational quotes, but rarely anchored in covenantal context. Scripture would become decorative—supporting a point rather than driving the discussion. Comment periods would remain surface-level, favoring personal affirmations that resonate emotionally, regardless of whether they teach revealed truth. Open-ended questions would elicit broad opinions, with little reference to the text at hand. Over time, this open-ended discussion-style approach would steamroll the gospel's doctrinal richness. Members may feel uplifted in the moment but remain unequipped for spiritual complexity, opposition, or confusion.

Talks and Lessons are Plagiarized

If scriptural illiteracy were to become widespread within the Church, one consequence would be the increasing use of pre-written, plagiarized, or AI-generated sacrament talks and lessons. While this may seem like a harmless shortcut amid busy lives, its implications are spiritually significant. It reflects a weakening of doctrinal fluency, a loss of confidence in personal scriptural interpretation, and a diminished sense of accountability to the revelatory process that should accompany gospel instruction. When members lack the habits or tools to study scripture meaningfully, they may turn to internet archives, blog posts, or language learning models to assemble talks that sound correct but are not spiritually or scripturally grounded. It would not be surprising if even official Church publications adopted this practice.

This concern has not gone unnoticed. In April 2025, Elder Ulisses Soares warned against the use of AI as a substitute for divine inspiration (_"Reverence for Sacred Things"_). While the tone was pastoral, the warning revealed a deeper concern—that members may outsource spiritual responsibility, bypassing the revelatory wrestle that should shape gospel teaching. As D&C 42:14 reminds us, "If ye receive not the Spirit ye shall not teach." Most concerning is that this trend signals a quiet lowering of spiritual expectations. When members believe doctrinal reflection is optional and instruction can be delegated to past talks or tools, the outward forms of Church life remain, but the inner power fades.

Gospel Language Becomes Sentimental or Therapeutic

If scriptural illiteracy were to become widespread within the Church, gospel language would start to shift from covenantal precision to therapeutic sentimentality. In such environments, the vocabulary of discipleship would be gradually redefined through cultural filters that prioritize comfort and affirmation over covenant and transformation.

This shift would become most evident in public discourse—lessons, testimonies, and informal expressions of faith. The gospel would be framed in terms of how it makes one feel, rather than what it requires. Phrases like "I know my Savior loves me" or "The gospel brings me peace" would replace more doctrinally rooted testimony. Words like *faith*, *grace*, and *repentance* would become buzzwords, increasingly softened and detached from their scriptural depth. Faith would become optimism. Grace would become tolerance. Repentance would become self-acceptance.

Fast and testimony meetings will be a good litmus test for this shift. In strong scriptural wards and stakes, testimonies will blend experience with doctrine, anchored in scripture and covenant. In less literate wards and stakes, testimonies will drift toward generalized gratitude and emotional uplift, with little reference to Christ's words or the Standard Works. Over time, those members will become fluent in *feeling* but illiterate in doctrine. Perhaps they would still be able to express impressions, but would be unable to explain or defend the truths those impressions are meant to reflect.

Reduced Ability to Identify Scriptural Patterns

If scriptural illiteracy were to become widespread within the Church, members would gradually lose the ability to recognize scriptural patterns. A defining feature of scripture is its use of symbolic and prophetic cycles—scattering and gathering, bondage and deliverance, apostasy and restoration, exile and return. These are the architectural logic of God's covenantal dealings. Scripturally fluent members see how these patterns play out not only in scripture, but in their own lives, families, and congregations. Where literacy is lacking, these patterns would remain completely obscured. Without these patterns, members would lose their interpretive tools. They would begin to navigate life through cultural or emotional frameworks rather than divine ones, and in doing so, trade the fullness of the gospel for fragments of the gospel.

Distorted Sense of Revelation

If scriptural illiteracy were to become widespread within the Church, there would be a distorted understanding of personal revelation. This would rarely manifest as overt apostasy, but rather as sincere misalignment—where spiritual impulses are no longer grounded in scriptural principles, doctrinal context, or prophetic safeguards. Over time, well-meaning members may mistake fleeting emotion for divine communication and develop a theology of revelation shaped more by internal impression than revealed truth.

A key symptom of this distortion would be the tendency to interpret emotional relief—such as the easing of anxiety or a sense of peace—as conclusive evidence of the Spirit. While the Holy Ghost does bring peace (Galatians 5:22), peace alone is not its only marker. John 14:26 describes the Spirit as one who teaches and brings truth to remembrance. Moroni 10:5 affirms that the Spirit reveals the truth of all things. Conversely, members may begin to assume that anything which feels good is divinely approved, and anything uncomfortable must be dismissed. But scripture is clear that the Spirit also corrects, reproves, and calls to repentance (see

Hebrews 12:6; D&C 1:27). In scripturally shallow environments, this broader understanding would be lost.

This drift would begin with gaps in gospel teaching. Saints would be taught to "follow the Spirit" without being taught *how* to test those promptings. Scripture mandates discernment (1 Thessalonians 5:21), yet without doctrinal fluency, members may assume spiritual impressions can override canon. In extreme cases, this leads to claims of personal revelation that conflict with Church teachings.

Stage 3 – Breakdown of Gospel Discernment
Starvation Stage: Cognitive Disintegration / Systemic Crisis

Moral Confusion or Over-Simplification

If scriptural illiteracy were to become widespread within the Church, one of the more spiritually disorienting consequences would be a decline in moral reasoning. The scriptures, when read canonically and contextually, present morality not as a checklist of behaviors but as a dynamic, covenantal process mediated through law, grace, prophecy, and divine timing. In scripturally literate communities, members learn to navigate moral ambiguity with wisdom drawn from divine patterns. Where this literacy fades, however, the ability to think ethically in revelatory terms fades with it.

In the absence of scriptural grounding, many members would default to rigid, binary moral categories—righteous versus wicked, obedient versus rebellious, etc. Moral judgments would become behavior-focused, often detached from context, prophetic exception, divine intention, or redemptive possibility. Complex questions about justice, mercy, paradox, or agency would be viewed with suspicion or avoided entirely. Furthermore, struggling members may be harshly judged, not through revealed standards, but through cultural tradition or personal bias. Others may mistake personal preference for eternal law or overlook true covenantal imperatives. This would create confusion and alienation in those seeking deeper discipleship.

Impaired Ability to Recognize Apostasy or Error

If scriptural illiteracy were to become widespread within the Church, members would gradually lose the ability to recognize apostasy, doctrinal error, or theological distortion. Members would adopt or tolerate ideas incompatible with revealed truth simply because they no longer recognize the boundaries established by scripture. Without scriptural discernment, ideas would be judged by tone or emotional resonance rather than doctrine. This would leave members vulnerable to speculative theology, mysticism, prosperity gospel, or cultural reinterpretations of truth.

Doctrinal passivity would play a major role in this. When members rely solely on manuals or secondhand interpretation, their spiritual immune system weakens. Charismatic voices may gain undue influence—not because they are true, but because they sound familiar to an untrained ear. The Book of Mormon specifically warns against this. Nephi and Alma speak of apostasy born not of rebellion, but forgetfulness and neglect (2 Nephi 28; Alma 12). Apostasy in such a setting doesn't storm in. It drifts in—unnoticed, unopposed, and unrecognized.

Doctrinal Confusion in the Home

If scriptural illiteracy were to become widespread within the Church, there would be a growing pattern of doctrinal confusion within the home. When parents lack scriptural confidence, when doctrinal engagement is outsourced to minimalistic Church programs, and when gospel conversations are shallow or absent, children are more likely to grow up with an unclear, simplistic, or distorted understanding of foundational truths.

This concern is especially pressing in light of the Church's "home-centered, Church-supported" model of learning, as emphasized in *Come, Follow Me*. That model assumes that parents *can* engage regularly and meaningfully with scripture. But when parents themselves are unfamiliar with the Standard Works—whether in content or interpretive method—they often feel unequipped to lead doctrinal discussions or answer hard questions. Family scripture study can become a brief, superficial ritual, avoiding complexity out of fear of "getting it wrong." In such homes, *Come, Follow Me* risks becoming a checklist—measuring participation by completion rather than comprehension. Children, in turn, learn that scripture is peripheral, complicated, or irrelevant.

Over time, this dynamic leads to quiet deconstruction. Children may associate gospel learning with boredom or vague sentimentality rather than transformation, guidance, or curiosity. When questions arise—as they inevitably do—parents may deflect or simplify, reinforcing the perception that the gospel has little to offer in the face of real struggle or complexity. In such a vacuum, other sources necessarily fill the interpretive gap. A child who has never seen their parents wrestle with scripture is unlikely to believe it holds answers. A home without doctrinal conversation becomes a home without doctrinal inheritance. This is rarely due to apathy, but to generational doctrinal insecurity. Many parents simply were never taught how.

Temple Worship Becomes Abstract or Confusing

If scriptural illiteracy were to become widespread within the Church, there would be a gradual disengagement from the meaning, coherence, and revelatory power of temple worship. Many members would continue to attend the temple out of duty, habit, or cultural expectation. But over time, temple worship would risk becoming abstract, confusing, or emotionally inaccessible because the scriptural framework that gives them meaning has faded from view.

Temple worship in the Church of Jesus Christ of Latter-day Saints is the culmination of covenantal patterns deeply rooted in scripture—especially in the Torah, Psalms, Isaiah, Hebrews, and Revelation. The layout of the temple, the sequence of ordinances, the covenants, clothing, and language—all draw on scriptural temple theology. When members cease to engage with the scriptures that inform these symbols, the temple loses its interpretive key.

The endowment, for example, finds parallels within Israel's tabernacle system, the high priest's ascent to the Holy of Holies, and apocalyptic visions in both canonical and apocryphal scripture. Covenants echo Deuteronomic structures of loyalty and renewal. Ordinances reenact creation, fall, atonement, and return. Without this scriptural architecture, members may sense the temple's importance but struggle to articulate or understand its content.

As a consequence of this, we would see many first-time temple attendees (particularly for initiatory/endowment ordinances) resign to treating these ordinances like Christian mysticism. Parents, teachers, and leaders would consistently "warn" new temple-goers that aspects of the experience might feel strange or confusing—largely because they themselves had never fully grasped its meaning. Over time, many members would quietly withdraw from temple attendance due to discomfort or detachment. Others would continue attending but feel mentally absent—unaware of the deeper meaning behind the rites. In all cases, the temple would cease to function as a source of doctrinal clarity and spiritual transformation, and become more akin to an idol.

A common symptom of this idolatry would be the confusion between secrecy and sacredness. Out of reverence—or uncertainty—many members would avoid discussing temple themes, even in appropriate settings such as gospel classrooms or family study. While very few specific elements of the temple are protected by secrecy, temple theology is not meant to be hidden. Prophets and apostles regularly teach temple doctrine publicly, but without scriptural knowledge, members would fail to recognize or internalize those teachings.

This would result in a kind of temple agnosticism. Members would affirm the temple's holiness but feel estranged from its meaning. They would say, "I know the temple is important," or "I feel peaceful while I'm there," but not really know why.

Stage 4 – Institutional and Cultural Erosion
Starvation Stage: Cachexia and Collapse / Terminal Shutdown

Over-Personalization of Scripture, Undermining Its Authority

If scriptural illiteracy were to become widespread within the Church, one of the more spiritually corrosive outcomes would be the over-personalization of scripture in ways that undermine its covenantal and revelatory authority. While personal application is essential to discipleship, reducing scripture primarily to individual insight can erode its role as divine instruction, prophetic witness, and binding declaration of God's will.

This tendency would be compounded by the mistaken belief that scripture was written for *us* in the modern day, rather than to ancient peoples in particular cultural and historical circumstances. Without a firm grasp of original context, members may project modern assumptions onto ancient texts, interpreting them solely through contemporary lenses.

This would often surface in classroom questions like, "What does this verse mean to you?" While inviting participation, such phrasing can unintentionally shift interpretation from covenantal fidelity to personal preference. Meaning would be judged by how a verse *feels*, not by what it declares. Lacking tools like historical context, canonical comparison, and doctrinal scaffolding, members would default to themselves. Scripture would become a vehicle for confirmation, not transformation.

Sacrament Meeting Becomes an Echo Chamber

If scriptural illiteracy were to become widespread within the Church, one outcome would be the gradual transformation of sacrament meeting into a space where discourse becomes circular and redundant rather than revelatory or scripturally grounded. Though sacrament meeting is not meant to be a doctrinal symposium, it is intended to center on Christ, reflect his teachings, and engage with revealed truth. When scripture no longer informs spiritual vocabulary, talks would draw not from canon, but from communal repetition.

This dynamic would be reinforced by rhetorical habits—"As Sister Smith said last week..." or "Like Brother Jones mentioned..." Talks would reference one another more than scripture or prophetic voice, forming a closed loop of communal validation. The scriptures would become purely decorative rather than directive. Over time, this would create a doctrinal monoculture where certain buzzwords dominate, while deeper concepts are either glossed over or simplified. In other words, orthodoxy would no longer be measured by scripture, but by repetition.

Missionary Work Becomes Emotionally-Driven

If scriptural illiteracy were to become widespread within the Church, there would be a shift in missionary work from doctrinal clarity to emotional appeal. While personal experience has always played a role in conversion, lasting discipleship depends on scriptural literacy, covenantal understanding, and doctrinal depth. When these foundations are weak, missionary work may appear fruitful but would lack staying power.

Where scripture is unfamiliar, missionary testimonies would be reduced to vague affirmations—"I know the Church is true because it brings peace," or "I feel good when I pray." These statements may be sincere, but without doctrinal scaffolding, they would leave investigators with emotional resonance and little theological substance. Converts would learn how to act, but not always what to believe or why.

As a result, conversion would become experiential rather than revelatory. When trials arise—or when alternate interpretations challenge beliefs— many would lack the doctrinal memory or spiritual vocabulary to remain anchored. This would have long-term consequences. Converts who join on emotion alone would struggle in Gospel Doctrine or temple preparation classes. They may quietly disengage, not from rebellion, but because they were never taught how to spiritually and doctrinally thrive.

Without the tools to grow, they would eventually slip away, unnoticed and unrooted.

Weak Retention and Conversion

If scriptural illiteracy were to become widespread within the Church, there would be a gradual weakening in both member retention and the durability of genuine conversion. Wards may still appear active, classes held, and programs functioning. But beneath the surface, a quiet erosion would be underway, disproportionately affecting converts, youth, and even returned missionaries. These members would struggle not from disbelief, but from never having "tasted the good word of God" (Hebrews 6:5) in a way that grounds and renews. Many of these members would inherit a secondhand testimony shaped more by cultural rhythm than personal conviction. The gospel, to them, may have felt more like expectations than revelation.

Data from the General Social Survey and Pew Research Center show declining Latter-day Saint retention over the past two decades. According to Pew's 2023-2024 Religious Landscape Study, only 54% of individuals raised in the Church of Jesus Christ of Latter-day Saints still identify with the faith as adults, a decrease from 70% in 2008. This retention rate is among the lowest for major U.S. religious groups, comparable to trends seen in Buddhist communities. The General Social Survey further reveals generational decline, with just 46% of Millennials raised LDS continuing their affiliation, compared to 62% among Generation X. Even among returned missionaries, approximately 40% are estimated to become inactive or leave—a sobering reality that challenges the assumption that missionary service guarantees long-term faithfulness. The evidence suggests deeper doctrinal formation is lacking, even among those once deeply involved.

Normalization of Dysfunction as the New Spiritual Baseline

If scriptural illiteracy were to become widespread within the Church, the most troubling consequence would be the collective failure to recognize these aforementioned deficiencies as problems at all. Over time, the accumulation of weakened gospel instruction, emotionalized conversion, and doctrinal vagueness would create a culture in which spiritual dysfunction becomes normalized as the new baseline. This is the most insidious outcome of scriptural illiteracy—not just the loss of knowledge, but the loss of awareness that something has even been lost.

And herein lies the essence of "active in the Church, but not active in the gospel." Programs may run, attendance remain steady, and teaching appear lively—yet the soul of discipleship is undernourished. A talk may feel "uplifting" without referencing Christ or scripture. A class may spark discussion without ever opening the assigned chapter. A member may say "I know the Church is true," but nothing of covenants, the Atonement of Christ, or the Restoration. This is the essence of dwindling in unbelief.

Chapter 4: Fed With Milk

There are undoubtedly many Latter-day Saints who will have read the previous chapter and found themselves deeply unsettled that the descriptions ring painfully familiar. For such individuals, the list of observed symptoms tied to scriptural illiteracy will not read as abstract theory or distant critique. It will instead reflect personal experience, ward culture, and spiritual atmosphere with an almost uncomfortable precision. I count myself among them. I have observed and lived most of these red flags firsthand. I see them in Church meetings every week.

The symptoms of spiritual hunger are not merely scattered, isolated anomalies. They appear to be widespread. In my view, the average stake of the Church of Jesus Christ of Latter-day Saints typically exists somewhere between stage 3 and stage 4 of spiritual starvation at any given time. And while this work focuses specifically on Latter-day Saints, I do not believe we are uniquely afflicted. These trends are discernible across many branches of modern Christianity, particularly in an era marked by accelerating secularism, intellectual fragmentation, and a growing cultural perception that God is increasingly distant or irrelevant.

For those who resonate with this assessment, it is only natural for questions to arise. When did this process of spiritual starvation begin? How did things progress to this point? Is there a tipping point beyond which recovery becomes impossible? What are the consequences of prolonged spiritual malnourishment? These are serious, urgent questions that deserve thoughtful, scripturally grounded reflection.

It is crucial to reemphasize that the majority of these challenges are not the result of malice, rebellion, or institutional betrayal. It would be a mistake to interpret the preceding chapter(s) as an accusation. In most cases, the underlying causes of doctrinal drift and scriptural disengagement are not sinister, but deeply human—rooted in neglect, fear, fatigue, misunderstanding, and cultural inertia. These problems are symptoms of spiritual starvation, and while their consequences are serious, their origins are often subtle, layered, and complex.

There are many reasons why Latter-day Saints may resist or avoid deeper engagement with the scriptures. For some, it is a fear of conflict—especially in a religious culture that emphasizes unity, harmony, and peace. For others, it may be a lingering discomfort from prior ecclesiastical or interpersonal trauma, where moments of theological tension or open questioning led to exclusion, misunderstanding, or pain. In such cases, deep study may feel threatening rather than life-giving.

Still others may avoid the scriptures due to a sense of inadequacy. The language of scripture—especially in the King James Bible and the Book of Mormon—can be challenging, filled with symbolism, historical references, and theological concepts that require effort and patience. Without sufficient scaffolding, members may conclude that scripture study is a task for the academically gifted or spiritually elite, rather than a divine inheritance accessible to all.

In some cases, members may have absorbed an unspoken culture of anti-intellectualism or doctrinal minimalism, where deep questions are dismissed as distractions from "what really matters" or are subtly pathologized as signs of spiritual pride. Phrases like "that won't affect your salvation" or "we just need to focus on Jesus" may, in context, reflect sincere concern, but they can also function as theological escape hatches—mechanisms for avoiding engagement rather than invitations to seek further light and knowledge.

I once heard a sister express her position in a moment of striking candor—"If I'm wrong about anything [re: faith/religion], I just don't want to know. I'm honestly more comfortable not knowing." This was a voice that had been conditioned to see spiritual complacency as faithfulness. And in truth, she was not an outlier. There are many like her. We have, in too many settings, cultivated a religious culture that does not hunger for the scriptures because it does not know what it is missing.

The Church of Jesus Christ of Latter-day Saints began as a profoundly scripture-focused organization. From its inception, prophetic instruction and congregational learning revolved around close reading of the Standard Works. It is only within the last two to three generations that the Church experienced a significant shift away from this scripture-heavy model of instruction. This gradual transition began to take shape in the mid-20th century, with its most noticeable developments emerging in the 1960s and accelerating thereafter. What follows is a brief historical overview tracing the evolution of Church teaching practices and the diminishing centrality of scripture in official curriculum.

In the early Restoration period, nearly all formal Church teaching centered directly on scripture. Sabbath School meetings in Kirtland and Nauvoo often featured scripture memorization and recitation. Sermons typically began with a scripture reading followed by interpretive commentary, a pattern influenced by Jewish midrashic tradition. Joseph Smith consistently emphasized the scriptures as the source of doctrinal authority, instructing elders to "preach the gospel…and to teach the gathering as set forth in the holy scriptures" (Ehat & Cook, "*The Words of Joseph Smith*," 1980). Scripture was not a backdrop. It *was* the curriculum.

During the pioneer era in Utah, the use of scripture remained prominent. The *Journal of Discourses* captured sermons in which Brigham Young and others routinely grounded their teachings in the Bible and Book of Mormon. Sunday School and Relief Society meetings were structured around reading and expounding scripture. While emphasis on modern prophetic guidance increased, the Church's instructional culture still treated the scriptures as the primary teaching texts.

In the early 20th century, the Church began systematizing its curricula under the direction of President Joseph F. Smith. The Correlation Program, initiated in the 1920s and expanded through the 1940s, aimed to coordinate teaching across the growing global Church. During this period, however, scriptural engagement remained robust. Seminary, Sunday School, and auxiliary manuals continued to be organized around the Standard Works. Correlation initially functioned to unify—not simplify—doctrinal teaching.

By the 1960s, a more substantial shift began. Correlation leadership increasingly focused on doctrinal principles over sequential scripture study. Home and Church curricula were restructured to strengthen family gospel teaching. In 1965, the first *Family Home Evening* manual was released, emphasizing practical application rather than scriptural exposition. Sunday meetings likewise began to prioritize gospel principles such as faith, repentance, and family unity. Though still anchored in scripture, the structure and tone of lessons moved from verse-by-verse study to topical reinforcement of core doctrines.

The 1970s saw the full institutionalization of Correlation. All Church curricula were brought under centralized oversight. A new four-year rotation was introduced to ensure systematic study of each of the Standard Works. While scripture remained central in name, teaching methods increasingly focused on summarizing doctrines rather than engaging deeply with text. Classes were designed to reinforce key gospel themes (e.g., Atonement, covenants) rather than explore entire scriptural narratives. Still, from 1972 to 1986, official instructions emphasized that the scriptures themselves were to serve as the student manuals, with teacher guides facilitating classroom discussion (El Call, *"A Timeline of LDS Sunday School Manuals,"* August 2022).

A major structural shift occurred in 1980 with the adoption of the three-hour block schedule. This consolidation—while efficient—reduced total teaching time for each class. In 1987, the Church introduced student manuals containing lesson summaries and commentary, replacing reliance on open scripture. For the first time since 1972, members were no longer directed to bring only their scriptures, but were given pre-outlined lessons. This marked the first real departure from a scripture-heavy model Church-wide. Lessons became increasingly simplified, emphasizing key takeaways and application rather than close textual engagement.

In 1998, the Church introduced the *Teachings of Presidents of the Church* series for Relief Society and Elders Quorum. These manuals compiled quotations from past prophets and organized them thematically. Scripture was referenced, but prophetic commentary took center stage. Simultaneously, youth and young adult programs shifted to topic-based instruction, further moving away from scriptural narrative in favor of lesson themes and personal stories. By the end of the 1990s, most Church instruction emphasized doctrinal application over scriptural exploration. This curriculum remained in use until the launch of *Come, Follow Me* in 2019.

This timeline highlights a gradual but definable arc from verse-centered teaching rooted in scripture to principle-based instruction guided by correlated manuals. The aim of this shift was clearly not to devalue scripture but to create unified, teachable content for a global Church. Nevertheless, it resulted in a reduction in scriptural fluency and exegetical depth across general Church curricula. Understanding this evolution is essential to recognizing both the strengths and limitations of the Church's current model.

There is no sole individual or isolated moment that singularly accounts for the modern Church's shift away from scripture-centered teaching. However, if one were to identify the most pivotal figure in this transition, President Harold B. Lee emerges as the most likely catalyst. While the formal Correlation movement began under the administration of President David O. McKay, it was Lee—then a member of the Quorum of the Twelve—who most forcefully articulated, designed, and implemented the structural transformation that would redefine Church teaching for generations.

President McKay, though revered for his spiritual vision and global outreach, had little appetite for administrative overhaul. He valued the home and expressed concern about rising secularism, but did not aggressively pursue curricular reform. Harold B. Lee, on the other hand, possessed a temperament suited to institutional engineering. Seeing widespread inconsistency in Church teaching—where auxiliaries operated semi-independently and sometimes taught conflicting interpretations of doctrine—Lee proposed a radical solution to centralize and correlate all instructional materials under First Presidency oversight.

This curricular realignment prioritized thematic consistency across age groups and auxiliaries, shifting from expository scripture study to principle-based instruction. The move was not merely instructional but cultural. Lee (and McKay, previously) were alarmed that Latter-day Saints were outsourcing spiritual education to Church programs, rather than taking responsibility for teaching the gospel at home. The 1965 formalization of Family Home Evening, with its accompanying manuals, underscored this concern. These materials emphasized practical gospel living, assuming that parents required simple frameworks rather than complex exegetical tools to reinforce doctrine.

Lee's broader cultural context helps explain his instincts. A product of the early 20th century, he was deeply shaped by technocratic modernism, a worldview that privileged efficiency, order, standardization, and hierarchical control. His leadership reflected the command structures of the military and the managerial rationalism of the postwar corporate world. In that light, his Correlation program mirrored contemporary trends in education, psychology, and bureaucracy. The Church, under his influence, came to resemble a streamlined institution, not unlike the federal government or Fortune 500 organizations—efficient, centralized, and message-controlled.

While Lee's reforms addressed real institutional needs, they also shifted the spiritual center of gravity. Gospel instruction became more accessible, but less scripturally rigorous. Manuals emphasized principles and summaries over passages and study. Over time, correlated teaching materials lost much of the prophetic texture and scriptural midrash that had characterized earlier Latter-day Saint discourse. In retrospect, what Lee envisioned as an inspired system for doctrinal clarity became, for some, a long-term trade-off—pedagogical coherence at the expense of doctrinal depth.

Interestingly, the prophets who followed Lee varied in how they related to this system. President Spencer W. Kimball, though approving of major Correlation fruits like the 1980 meeting block and revised missionary discussions, remained a deeply scripture-focused leader. His hallmark works—*The Miracle of Forgiveness* (1969) and *Faith Precedes the Miracle* (1972)—exhibit a robust, scripture-saturated tone, and his calls to repentance were rooted in prophetic seriousness. Ezra Taft Benson, his successor, went even further in calling the Church back to the scriptures. His famous 1986 charge to "flood the earth with the Book of Mormon" was a direct response to scriptural neglect and an implicit critique of what Correlation had inadvertently produced. Yet even Benson could not reverse the system. By the late 1980s, Correlation was not just a program—it was the operating system of the Church.

The three presidents who followed—Howard W. Hunter, Gordon B. Hinckley, and Thomas S. Monson—seemed to have fully embraced the correlated Church as the world they had inherited. President Hunter, though briefly in office, emphasized temple worship and did not meaningfully engage with curricula. President Hinckley expanded institutional infrastructure, accelerated global reach, and trusted the existing doctrinal system to serve the Church's needs. His teachings emphasized clarity, warmth, and missionary appeal—tones that worked well in a correlated environment. President Monson, likewise, modeled a ministry of pastoral care and personal testimony, focusing on ministering, humanitarian service, and spiritual uplift. None of these leaders expressed concern about the effects of Correlation, perhaps because none of them really knew a Church without it.

That final observation is essential. Spencer W. Kimball and Ezra Taft Benson were both born in the 19th century—into a Church still shaped by men who had known Joseph Smith and Brigham Young. They inherited a culture of raw prophetic intensity and deep scriptural engagement. In contrast, Presidents Hunter, Hinckley, and Monson were born into the early 20th-century Church—a Church already moving toward centralization and experiencing the spiritual consequences of institutional drift. Their experience of the Church was not one of shift or loss, but stability and continuity. What may have felt to Benson like a crisis of scriptural illiteracy may have seemed, to his successors, like normalcy.

In light of the concerns and historical developments outlined thus far, it is both necessary and fair to acknowledge that many members of the Church of Jesus Christ of Latter-day Saints may respond to this analysis by pointing to the substantial institutional efforts the Church has undertaken in recent years to reinvigorate scriptural engagement—most notably through the introduction of the *Come, Follow Me* curriculum. This response is not only valid but warrants thoughtful and respectful consideration, particularly in view of the program's scope, design, and explicitly stated aims.

Launched in 2019 and designed to support a "home-centered, Church-supported" model of gospel learning, Come, Follow Me represents one of the most ambitious and far-reaching efforts in the modern history of the Church to return scripture study to the heart of daily discipleship. The shift in emphasis—from classroom-based instruction to home-centered learning—signals a significant reorientation of responsibility, moving gospel teaching away from institutional dependency and into the hands of families and individuals. This reflects a deep conviction that the spiritual vitality of the Saints must be rooted in personal and familial engagement with the word of God.

In practical terms, the Come, Follow Me materials have made scripture study more accessible to a wider range of learners. Weekly lessons are organized around the Standard Works, paired with questions for reflection, historical context, cross-references, and opportunities for application. The design is both modular and adaptable, allowing families of varying sizes, ages, and spiritual maturity to tailor their study to their own needs and capacities. For many members, Come, Follow Me has facilitated a more consistent rhythm of scripture engagement than ever before, especially among those who had previously relied almost exclusively on Sunday instruction for their spiritual nourishment. In this sense, Come, Follow Me could be viewed as a strength of the Church's current approach to scriptural education.

Having introduced the Come, Follow Me curriculum in good faith—as a meaningful and institutionally commendable shift— it is now appropriate to undertake a more critical and evaluative examination of its structure and outcomes. While the aims of the curriculum are clearly stated and widely affirmed, there remains legitimate concern about whether the materials themselves, in both form and content, are robust enough to sustain the kind of scriptural literacy and doctrinal depth the Church claims to seek.

First, it is important to acknowledge that the Come, Follow Me manuals are structured as concise outlines rather than comprehensive lessons. This represents a significant departure from prior instructional models. For example, the pre-2019 Gospel Doctrine teacher manuals often began with extended introductions with historical vignettes, doctrinal commentary, and quotations from General Authorities or Church historians. These lessons were designed to fill a full class hour with structured instruction. In contrast, Come, Follow Me materials provide brief introductions, a selection of scripture passages, and a few open-ended discussion questions. As explained in one Church-produced FAQ, the curriculum "does not prescribe everything you should say and do in class…it suggests scriptures and other resources to help you learn the doctrine for yourself, followed by a few ideas to help learners discover the doctrine for themselves" (Church of Jesus Christ, "*Come, Follow Me for Training Teachers and Leaders*"). This reflects a deliberate shift from instructor-led exposition to learner-guided discovery.

On the surface, this might appear empowering. The curriculum assumes that members will take greater responsibility for their own gospel learning. Yet there is an inherent tension between accessibility and depth. The result is a set of materials that shorten and simplify both lesson preparation and reading load. A typical Come, Follow Me week now focuses on a small selection of verses or a single theme, and as of 2024, youth and adult classes have been further streamlined to use a single unified manual per quarter—*Come, Follow Me: For Home and Church*. This simplification does increase accessibility, but it also risks reducing doctrinal richness.

A comparison with previous manuals is informative, to say the least. For instance, the Doctrine and Covenants and Church History manual(s) included extensive commentary and historical background across multiple pages. Doctrinal insights were embedded directly into the text, and the structure of lessons often reflected a topical or sequential approach to scripture that assumed a baseline familiarity with key theological frameworks. In Come, Follow Me, that kind of scaffolding is largely omitted. The doctrinal content is now meant to be inferred, rather than stated, leaving it to the teacher or learner to supplement with additional resources. For some, this flexibility is welcome. But for others, especially those without extensive background in scripture or theology, it may result in ambiguity or doctrinal shallowness.

Church leaders have acknowledged this risk. One official source describes the new method as a "new way of learning" and compares scripture study to a treasure hunt, where learners must "dig a bit" to find spiritual insights (Church of Jesus Christ, "*Learning a New Way of Learning*"). While the metaphor is well-intentioned, it invites a difficult question—Why should spiritual nourishment, so often likened by Christ himself to physical nourishment, require concealment? When the soul is hungry, why must it dig through outlines and optional questions in the hope of discovering doctrinal substance?

This concern becomes even more acute when one considers the shift in institutional structure that accompanied the rollout of Come, Follow Me. In 2019, the Church reduced its weekly Sunday block from three hours to two, eliminating a full hour formerly dedicated to Gospel Doctrine instruction. While adult Sunday School has since been partially restored on a rotating basis, the time available for structured, teacher-led scriptural instruction has effectively been halved. President Mark L. Pace, formerly of the Sunday School General Presidency, reinforced the new direction, emphasizing that the "best thing" a teacher can do is leave students feeling motivated to study the scriptures at home. This comment is very telling that the Church now views Sunday instruction as a supplement to, rather than the foundation of, scriptural learning. Of course, this is not without precedent. It is, in fact, reminiscent of David O. McKay's concern that Church programs could overshadow individual and family responsibility for spiritual instruction.

However, this model assumes that members *are* compensating for reduced class time with increased home study. But this is, frankly, a precarious assumption. Anecdotally and statistically, many families and individuals do not engage with the Come, Follow Me curriculum on a daily—or even weekly—basis. For those who lack strong habits of home study or who are spiritually undernourished to begin with, this shift has functioned less like an invitation and more like a quiet withdrawal of institutional support. The curriculum's self-directed model assumes a level of motivation and scriptural confidence that, for many, simply does not exist.

To illustrate the real-world implications—assuming a generous 40 minutes of supplementary scripture study in each of the 26 weeks that adult Sunday School meets (accounting for stake conferences, holidays, or ward meetings), and assuming perfect attendance, members would receive just over 17 hours of institutional scripture study per year. In practice, this number is likely much lower. For many, this is all the scriptural exposure they receive. Combined with the often-therapeutic tone of sacrament meetings (as discussed in the previous chapter), the average member's spiritual formation is being carried by just a handful of hours per year of shared scriptural learning—less than is even required for continuing education in many professional fields.

To be clear, the Come, Follow Me initiative is not inherently deficient. It represents an important and inspired effort to foster greater personal responsibility in gospel learning. But the shift to a home-centered model without adequately accounting for the literacy of its membership has created a pedagogical gap that risks widening unless directly addressed. A curriculum that is "principle-focused" may indeed help learners internalize key doctrines, but it also risks skipping over the nuance, complexity, and historical rootedness that has traditionally given Latter-day Saint theology its distinctive depth.

If the ultimate goal is deeper conversion to Christ—as the First Presidency has declared, and as stated explicitly in every publication of Come, Follow Me, including its early beta versions in the Church's digital archives—then that aim must be measured not only by increased flexibility or participation, but by increased understanding. It must be rooted in covenant, nourished by the word, and shaped by the whole counsel of God (Acts 20:27).

It is important to recognize that prior to 2019, many Gospel Doctrine classes, auxiliary programs, and family-based study efforts operated with a patchwork of manuals—despite nearly five decades of the Correlation movement. In this regard, the Come, Follow Me project represents a significant improvement. Even a brief review of the digital archives—dated back to 2013—makes clear that this initiative was not hastily assembled. It reflects over a decade of careful, deliberate work directed from the highest levels of Church leadership. By consolidating instructional efforts across all age groups and harmonizing the rhythm of gospel study Churchwide, Come, Follow Me introduces a level of curricular unity that is arguably unprecedented in the modern history of the Church.

However, this strength of standardization must be held in balance with more sobering questions about the doctrinal content and intellectual demands of the current curriculum. While past materials were far from perfect, as has been established in this chapter, they often assumed, and therefore fostered, a greater level of doctrinal engagement and theological rigor than much of what is now offered in standard Church instruction.

Take, for instance, the widely used *The Life and Teachings of Jesus and His Apostles* manual, which served as the New Testament institute curriculum from 1979 into the early 2000s. This text offered extensive verse-by-verse exegesis, historical contextualization, and cross-references to modern and ancient scripture. Doctrinal application was paired with rigorous textual analysis, and the manual frequently drew upon General Authorities, early Christian thinkers, and even respected Protestant theologians to enrich understanding. It was virtually the only resource of its kind during a period when the Correlation movement had largely stripped scriptural complexity from other Church program manuals. It was a demanding resource far denser and more intellectually robust than the comparatively brief and question-driven format of Come, Follow Me.

It's also worth mentioning that many Latter-day Saints in the 1980s and 1990s encountered doctrinal depth through the de facto influence of figures such as Elder Neal A. Maxwell and President Ezra Taft Benson. Maxwell's General Conference addresses were widely quoted in seminary, institute, and Gospel Doctrine settings and offered an elevated scriptural vocabulary. Benson, meanwhile, had invoked a Church-wide emphasis on the Book of Mormon, warning against modern Gadiantonism, materialism, and institutional decline. These teachings demanded critical thought and reflection on difficult themes, including pride, prophetic rejection, and apostasy. Their cultural influence helped elevate the level of doctrinal seriousness within the broader Church, irrespective of the influence of the Correlation movement.

The intellectual atmosphere of religious education during this period was further reinforced by materials produced and assigned at Brigham Young University. Through the 1990s and early 2000s, many undergraduate religion courses required substantive readings and theological texts. Students engaged with the lectures of Truman Madsen, doctrinal commentaries by Bruce R. McConkie, and extensive selections from

Hugh Nibley, James E. Talmage, John A. Widtsoe, and others. These sources often demanded careful interpretive attention, assumed a mature doctrinal vocabulary, and refused to dilute complex teachings for the sake of accessibility. Importantly, these resources were not confined to academia alone—they often shaped seminary, institute, and Gospel Doctrine discourse throughout the Church.

Even the *Teachings of Presidents of the Church* offered members a more historically grounded and doctrinally nuanced engagement with the faith, despite overt reduction of scriptural exegesis. These manuals certainly did not shy away from complex or challenging topics. They occasionally included bold teachings—Joseph Fielding Smith's commentary on apostasy, or Brigham Young's uncompromising views on obedience and sacrifice—that reflected the intellectual and theological priorities of their time. Members were not merely encouraged to extract broad principles, but asked to engage deeply with the actual words and ideas of prophets whose voices, though less familiar to modern Saints, formed the backbone of Restoration theology.

By comparison, the Come, Follow Me materials, though based on the Standard Works, are more principle-focused and significantly less analytical, offering simplified summaries and exploratory questions rather than sustained doctrinal exposition. While the flexibility and accessibility of Come, Follow Me may meet the needs of a broader spectrum of learners, it also risks flattening theological complexity and cultivating generations of Saints less equipped to wrestle with scripture or articulate the intricacies of their faith.

This leads us to what is perhaps the most difficult aspect of the Come, Follow Me program. While many members of the Church may regard it as a modernized teaching aid or a practical curricular refinement, it is essential to recognize that the program was introduced—and explicitly framed—by the First Presidency and the Quorum of the Twelve Apostles in *revelatory* terms, particularly within the context of the October 2018 General Conference. From its initial announcement to its ongoing implementation, Come, Follow Me has been consistently described not merely as a product of committee or administration, but as the result of divine inspiration received through God's ordained servants. The tone of official communications surrounding the curriculum, as well as its rollout and reception, indicate that members are expected to regard the program as more than organizational improvement—it is intended to be embraced as inspired, perhaps even prophetic, instruction for our time.

This framing is theologically significant because it redefines how faithful Latter-day Saints are meant to evaluate and respond to the curriculum. If Come, Follow Me is the fruit of revelation, then its adoption becomes a matter not only of educational policy but of covenantal alignment. For those with deep reverence for prophetic leadership, this imposes a sacred obligation to take the curriculum seriously in spirit and practice.

In the interest of transparency and doctrinal integrity, I must now address a tension that may be difficult but necessary. To speak plainly— while Come, Follow Me represents a step forward in certain respects, particularly in its increased emphasis on the Standard Works, it also constitutes, in my view, a significant regression in several far more critical areas, which this chapter has sought to examine in depth. Namely:

> *True Engagement.* The curriculum often lacks the scaffolding necessary to foster deep doctrinal wrestling or textual exploration. It presumes, rather than cultivates, scriptural fluency.

> *Doctrinal Depth.* Compared to previous curricula, Come, Follow Me offers significantly less exposition, historical framing, or theological commentary.

> *Church-Supported Learning.* The pivot to home-centered study has resulted in a substantial reduction in structured, teacher-led instruction, placing heavy reliance on self-directed learning without sufficient institutional support.

Symbolic and Canonical Integration. The curriculum frequently omits opportunities to explore cross-scriptural patterns, covenantal typologies, or even temple symbolism that would enrich doctrinal understanding.

Theological Confidence. By minimizing explicit doctrinal explanation, the curriculum often leaves interpretation almost entirely to the learner, which may inadvertently foster uncertainty or theological minimalism.

To be clear, these critiques are not offered as a rejection of the idea that Come, Follow Me is inspired. I do not assert that the curriculum is devoid of revelation. What I am suggesting, however, is that the form of that revelation may be preparatory rather than complete. Come, Follow Me may function as a sort of framework, a first iteration intended to establish individual and familial responsibility for gospel learning. But as it currently stands, it is difficult to see how its structure alone could achieve the kind of deep scriptural literacy, doctrinal resilience, and covenantal understanding that the Restoration demands in an increasingly secular world.

Thus, I find myself asking an honest and perhaps uncomfortable question—In *what* sense is this curriculum revealed? If we believe that "man shall not live by bread alone, but by every word that proceedeth out of the mouth of God" (Matthew 4:4), then we must be willing to interrogate whether the curriculum, in both content and method, provides the substantive nourishment that the Saints require. We must allow for the possibility that inspiration can manifest incrementally, that it may begin with a simplified structure meant to awaken spiritual habits, but that further refinement may be urgently needed.

In this sense, I do not necessarily reject Come, Follow Me. I regard it as an inspired starting point—but certainly not a sufficient endpoint. Like many of the Church's programs, policies, and educational tools throughout history, it may require continual revelation, correction, and expansion to meet the deepening needs of a spiritually maturing people. Revelation, after all, is not static. It is line upon line (2 Nephi 28:30). And it is precisely because we take seriously the prophetic claim of inspiration that we must be willing to engage the curriculum not only with loyalty, but with holy yearning for something richer, fuller, and more capable of transforming not just habits, but hearts.

For the spiritually hungry, the disillusioned, and the reflective Latter-day Saint, a natural and pressing question arises—*How are we to reconcile the portrayal of the current scriptural curriculum as revelatory and inspired, with the observable reality that its content often feels preliminary, minimalistic, or lacking in doctrinal depth?* In other words, how does one make sense of the fact that Church leadership presents Come, Follow Me not as a transitional or preparatory measure, but as a fully realized curriculum, designed, implemented, and sustained by revelation for the purpose of drawing individuals and families closer to the Savior?

To date, there has been no official acknowledgment that the curriculum is in any way incomplete or intentionally introductory. On the contrary, public statements and institutional messaging have consistently framed Come, Follow Me as the divinely appointed tool to guide the Saints in deepening their conversion, enriching their homes, and fortifying their discipleship. So, for those who resonate with the critiques offered in this work, this framing creates an understandable tension. How, one may ask, could a curriculum so clearly reduced in theological scaffolding and exegetical substance be the product of revelation?

My response to that question, though admittedly uncomfortable, is one I offer with sincerity and transparency—the Church does not always get it right. This is not an indictment, but a recognition of a deeply embedded doctrinal truth affirmed repeatedly by prophetic leadership. Prophets are not infallible. The Church of Jesus Christ of Latter-day Saints does not hold that its leaders are incapable of error. On the contrary, multiple prophets and apostles have explicitly acknowledged that mistakes can be made in the administration of the Church, especially in matters of policy, interpretation, or curricular design.

One of the clearest areas in which this principle becomes visible is in the historically fluid boundary between doctrine and policy. In theory, eternal doctrines are immutable, while policies and programs are subject to change according to the needs of the Church and the ongoing reception of revelation. In practice, however, the distinction has often been ambiguous, with policies gradually acquiring the weight of doctrine due to their longevity, rhetorical framing, or institutional emphasis. The difficulty for members lies in the fact that when a prophet teaches—even on matters of policy—the teaching is often received as doctrine, especially when it is described in revelatory terms.

A brief survey of historical examples bears this out:

- Plural Marriage was once introduced as a divinely revealed doctrine essential to exaltation (D&C 132), publicly defended by Church leaders for decades. When President Wilford Woodruff issued the 1890 Manifesto under legal and political duress, it was framed not as a reversal of doctrine, but a change in practice. Nevertheless, this change fractured many Saints' sense of theological continuity, leading to splinter groups that continue the practice to this day.

- The priesthood and temple restriction for Black members, while originally a policy, was reinforced for over a century through doctrinal justifications—including speculative theology about premortal neutrality and divine cursing. Its reversal in 1978, through Official Declaration 2, required not only policy change but an implicit re-evaluation of many long-standing teachings. The painful legacy of that change is still being navigated today.

- The 2015 baptism policy, which barred the children of same-sex couples from receiving Church ordinances until age 18 and classified same-sex marriage as apostasy, was publicly described as revelatory by then-President of the Quorum of the Twelve, Russell M. Nelson. Yet less than four years later, the policy was rescinded. No doctrinal rationale was ever fully provided for the reversal, leaving many members—on all sides of the issue—confused or spiritually disoriented.

- Other examples, such as the discontinuation of women's healing blessings, the former prohibition on women praying in sacrament meetings, and the eventual denunciation of Brigham Young's Adam-God doctrine (which was formerly taught at the temple veil), further illustrate how inspired policies, and indeed even doctrines, have been revised, corrected, or disavowed over time, despite once being presented with confidence and spiritual authority.

These examples are not brought forward to erode trust in prophetic leadership. Rather, they invite us to embrace a mature, covenantal discipleship that can sustain both reverent loyalty to Church leaders and a clear-eyed awareness that human fallibility coexists with prophetic authority. As Latter-day Saints, we are called not to suspend spiritual discernment, but to exercise it within the bounds of faith.

Let me be unequivocally clear—I fully sustain the First Presidency and the Quorum of the Twelve Apostles as prophets, seers, and revelators. I affirm that the President of the Church of Jesus Christ of Latter-day Saints is the only person on earth authorized to exercise all priesthood keys. And I hold that conviction not lightly, but with reverence and deep personal testimony.

At the same time, I believe that disciples of Jesus Christ are invited—indeed, commanded—to "test all things" (1 Thessalonians 5:21), to "search the scriptures" (John 5:39), and to cultivate the kind of spiritual literacy that allows us to discern the Lord's voice even when spoken through fallible vessels. This posture does not represent rebellion. It is the very essence of covenantal accountability.

It is in this spirit that I have arrived at what I can only describe as a personal spiritual conviction that the Church's movement away from scripture-rich, analytically rigorous gospel instruction toward a devotional, principle-centered model constitutes a profound misstep. I do not believe this shift is the result of malice or incompetence. Rather, I believe it may be a well-intentioned adaptation to a series of questionable decisions made by a long line of preceding prophets—an adaptation that, however inadvertently, deprives rising generations of the very doctrinal tools it needs to remain spiritually resilient in an increasingly post-Christian world.

If this shift was indeed revealed, then we are faced with a sobering possibility that the Lord himself is permitting a season of spiritual minimalism among his people for reasons not yet made manifest. Scripture does contain certain precedents for this—a preparatory law given in times of rebellion (as in Moses' law), or a famine of the word prophesied by Amos. But if this is such a time, then it deserves to be named, acknowledged, and wrestled with—not quietly normalized under the guise of progress.

The Church's own leaders have long emphasized the primacy of scripture in building testimony. In his final General Conference address, President Thomas S. Monson pleaded with the Saints to immerse themselves in the Book of Mormon. This call was not rhetorical. It was urgent. And any shift in curriculum that diminishes the quantity and quality of scriptural engagement across all four Standard Works ultimately undercuts that prophetic charge.

The modern instructional model of "home-centered, Church-supported" is widely embraced by Church leadership and adopted into the Come, Follow Me curriculum. In the words of a note to teachers from the Come, Follow Me 2025 Manual—"keep in mind that learning the gospel, at its best, is home centered and church supported. In other words, your main responsibility is to support the people you teach in their efforts to learn and live the gospel at home. Don't worry about having unique content to provide for them in class. Instead, give them opportunities to share their experiences, thoughts, and questions about the scripture passages they've read at home...This is more important than covering a certain amount of material." However, this raises a critical ecclesiological question—in what *precise* ways is the Church meaningfully *supporting* gospel learning?

The Come, Follow Me curriculum is often described as a supplemental resource. However, this characterization rests on the assumption that there exists a primary source of spiritual nourishment to which it is supplemental. But if structured, substantive teaching within the Church has been minimized or altogether decentralized, then what exactly is being supplemented? A supplement implies the presence of a foundational core, but in many wards and branches, what currently exists feels more akin to replacement than to reinforcement. Thus, one must ask whether the Church is truly *supporting* gospel learning, or rather *deflecting* from institutional responsibility under the banner of familial autonomy.

To be clear, this critique is not directed specifically at the present administration or at President Russell M. Nelson, under whom the "home-centered, Church-supported" language has been reinvigorated. Rather, the ideological roots of this model trace back to President David O. McKay, who famously taught, "No other success can compensate for failure in the home." That phrase, often cited with reverence, became something of a philosophical north star for generations of Church instruction. It emerged during a critical inflection point in American religious and political life. That era was defined by Cold War anxieties, the ideological clash between Western Christianity and Soviet atheism, and a robust cultural defense of traditional family structures.

President McKay was an ardent anti-communist, and his emphasis on the home as the nucleus of moral instruction cannot be divorced from that broader context. In an age where national identity, religious conviction, and anti-communist patriotism were increasingly interwoven, the home became a symbolic battleground for preserving liberty, civilization, and Christian virtue. McKay's call to strengthen the home reflected a genuine desire to safeguard the rising generation from secularism and moral erosion.

In fairness, it is difficult to critique historical decisions without acknowledging the unique pressures of their time. I did not grow up under the specter of global communism. I have not experienced the existential fear of ideological conquest or cultural collapse. In that light, McKay's vision was likely a sincere, context-driven effort to empower families in a rapidly changing world.

Yet while the historical motivations may be understandable, the theological implications remain deeply problematic when such a model is adopted *indefinitely* and without balance. A sustained reliance on "home-centered" instruction as the dominant framework for gospel learning stands in tension not only with the early restored Church but with the teachings and structure of Christ's ministry itself.

The early Church of Jesus Christ of Latter-day Saints was distinctly *church-centered* in both philosophy and practice. Instructional models such as the Kirtland School of the Prophets, the Relief Society under Joseph Smith, the organization of priesthood quorums, and the robust doctrinal training given in formal gatherings all demonstrate a pattern of centralized, communal, and ecclesiastically-led teaching. Zion, as envisioned by the early Saints, was not an abstract idea realized within individual households—it was to be built through gathered communities under priesthood direction, nourished by shared doctrine and united covenants.

Joseph Smith's revelations did not delegate spiritual instruction solely to families. They formalized it within the institutional Church. Sections such as Doctrine and Covenants 20 and 88 assign teaching responsibilities to quorums, councils, and presidencies—not merely as administrators, but as teachers "watching over the church always" and "instructing" members in doctrine and duty. In this model, ecclesiastical leaders are explicitly tasked with providing spiritual nourishment, just as Christ commanded.

And it is here that the most striking tension emerges. In John 21:15–17, the resurrected Christ thrice commands Peter, a representative of apostolic leadership, to "Feed my lambs" and "Feed my sheep." These imperatives are not optional. They are urgent, personal commissions following Peter's declaration of love for the Savior. The commandment to feed implies active nourishment, attentiveness, and pastoral care. Nowhere in the text does Christ suggest the sheep should be taught to fend for themselves or to receive sustenance solely from within the flock. If one unfamiliar with Christianity were to read a Come, Follow Me manual in isolation, they might reasonably infer that Christ's directive had become "Teach the sheep to feed themselves."

Such a shift ought to concern any serious disciple. The shepherding metaphor used by Christ, and expanded upon in later epistles, implies proximity, accountability, and intervention. The ecclesiastical structure of the New Testament affirms this model with apostles, bishops, elders, and teachers assigned to "watch over the flock" (Acts 20:28), to "preach the word...in season and out of season" (2 Timothy 4:2), and to guard against doctrinal instability and spiritual drift (Ephesians 4:14). In the earliest Christian communities, the Church was not a secondary support system for private family devotion. It *was* the conduit through which discipleship was taught, reinforced, and lived.

It should also be said that a home-centered model, when overly emphasized, inevitably creates inequity within the body of Christ. Families differ drastically in spiritual capacity, doctrinal literacy, and consistency. Many faithful members come from broken, inactive, doctrinally shallow, or non-LDS households. For them, the Church may be the only reliable source of spiritual instruction. When the burden of gospel teaching is shifted entirely to the home, these individuals are effectively left behind, not by apostasy, but by neglect.

"Home-centered, Church-supported" was not the model instituted by Christ.

Allow me to restate that point for the sake of absolute clarity and gravity.

"Home-centered, Church-supported" was not the model instituted by Christ.

And anyone who insists otherwise is, in effect, demonstrating the very kind of scriptural illiteracy under discussion.

Christ ministered to the one and structured his Church to ensure no member was left without access to spiritual nourishment. A truly Church-centered system offers spiritual egalitarianism, ensuring that all, regardless of their circumstances, receive consistent and substantive doctrinal teaching through communal worship, organized instruction, and pastoral care.

This is cause for sober reflection. Just as ancient Israel came to love the scaffolding of the law more than the Lawgiver himself, are we in danger of becoming too content with what was meant to be transitional? Have we mistaken accessibility for sufficiency? Have we exchanged theological literacy for devotional familiarity? These are questions offered in love, and in the hope that we may yet reclaim the deep scriptural inheritance entrusted to the covenant people of God.

The following chapter will explore what I believe to be the probable long-term consequences of the current instructional paradigm within the Church of Jesus Christ of Latter-day Saints. But before proceeding, it seems fitting to address what may be a lingering question in the reader's mind throughout this work—Why does any of this matter so much to me? Why invest so much energy, attention, and even criticism into an organization I profess to love? Why risk rocking the boat?

Some readers, having followed the argument thus far, may feel inclined to respond with a degree of resignation or relativism: *Good for you. You clearly have a deep love for the scriptures and a higher understanding of gospel learning.*

But that doesn't mean everyone must approach it the same way. Everyone learns differently. Everyone grows at their own pace. Indeed, one might even cite Elder David A. Bednar's well-known "Patterns of Light" discourse as an apologetic defense of the view that spiritual understanding comes through diverse means, in diverse times, and by the Lord's design.

That is not in dispute.

But such appeals, while comforting on the surface, often function as rhetorical diversions, disarming the urgency of serious institutional critique by appealing to general truths. Yes, people learn differently. Yes, spiritual insight unfolds at varied rates. But this does not excuse systemic malnourishment. Nor does it resolve the central concern—What if the very institution meant to nourish souls is contributing to their spiritual starvation?

The reason I care so deeply is simply because I do not want the Church to be the reason we are losing people, particularly our youth. I do not want the Church, through its own curricular inadequacies or pedagogical assumptions, to be complicit in the steady erosion of testimony. Christ's warning in Matthew 18:6 should haunt us to our core—"But whoso shall offend one of these little ones which believe in me, it were better for him that a millstone were hanged about his neck, and that he were drowned in the depth of the sea." The Greek term used here for "offend" (*skandalísē*) implies a stumbling block—something that causes another to fall away. This is not a casual warning. It is a sobering indictment.

As this work has attempted to establish, the current generation of Latter-day Saint youth is not receiving adequate spiritual nourishment, particularly when it comes to scriptural literacy. They are not consistently encountering the scriptures in Primary. They are not being deeply engaged with the word in Sunday School. They are not being formed by the text in seminary, or in institute, or even at Church-sponsored institutions of higher learning. They are not receiving it in the Missionary Training Center. And when they become adults, many do not receive it during their Sabbath experience either.

To borrow a phrase often used in the performing arts world—"You *do* the show you know." In other words, the way one practices is the way one performs. If gospel instruction during a person's formative years consists largely of superficial discussions, handout-driven devotionals, and oversimplified moral adages loosely attached to scripture, then that is the "show" they will continue to perform as adults. If they have never been fed spiritually—if they have never learned to feast upon the word— they will not magically begin doing so on their own. They will not become powerful gospel instructors in the home. They will perpetuate the pattern they have internalized.

And this, I argue, is precisely what is happening.

The children we are raising to be content with scriptural illiteracy will one day become the leaders of that same system—leaders who will continue to teach and administer within a structure that no longer knows how to nourish the flock. In this way, we are witnessing generations of starving sheep raising more starving sheep, until eventually no one remembers what spiritual nourishment ever felt like. And all the while, we will look around and wonder why we are so hungry…

The reason I care so much, perhaps to the point of obsession, is because those around me often treat this hunger as some great unsolvable mystery. It is not. It's not mysterious at all.

We lament the increasing number of young people leaving the Church. We organize conferences, publish studies, and deliver talks to diagnose the trend. But have we paused just for a moment to consider the possibility that the system itself bears some responsibility? That we may be losing them because we fed them milk for years, spoonful by spoonful, and then one day they encountered something in Church history, or in policy, or even in the scriptures themselves, that required real spiritual muscle…and they didn't have it. They hadn't been trained to wrestle. They hadn't been taught how to reason through contradiction, to endure nuance, to seek personal revelation in the face of complexity.

And what happens then?

Many feel betrayed—left to wonder if they were deceived or simply unprepared. Some question whether they ever had a testimony at all. Others lose the ability to discern the Spirit amidst the din of disillusionment. And for those of us who have been in the Church long enough, we know how this usually ends. A long, slow disengagement. A quiet withdrawal. Sometimes a sudden break. And eventually, the only plausible path back into the fold lies through fond memories, the grace of circumstance, profound kindness from others, and, frankly, a lot of prayer.

That is a brutally unfair way to treat the rising generation. It is spiritual starvation disguised as pastoral care. And it could have been prevented.

I'm convinced it still can be.

Chapter 5: Dwindling in Unbelief

In response to the concerns raised regarding the decline in scriptural literacy and the shift toward simplified curriculum models, there are many faithful and well-meaning Latter-day Saints who might respond with a sense of reassurance: *If things were really going wrong, the Lord would intervene.* This sentiment, though grounded in faith, reflects a dangerous form of theological presumption. It reveals a subtle yet critical misunderstanding of the role of divine stewardship and of the patterns by which the Lord operates among his covenant people.

The Restoration affirms that God has called the Saints not to passive belief, but to active stewardship over the revealed word, sacred ordinances, and the covenants of the gospel. Christ himself taught explicitly on the weight of such stewardship through parables—the Parable of the Talents (Matthew 25:14–30) and the Parable of the Ten Virgins (Matthew 25:1–13) both emphasize personal accountability in spiritual preparation and fidelity to entrusted truth. Likewise, his warning that "If the salt have lost his savour, wherewith shall it be salted? it is thenceforth good for nothing" (Matthew 5:13) is a direct indictment of covenant holders who abandon their distinctive mission and cease to act as preserving agents in a decaying world.

These teachings underscore a vital theological reality that God does not intervene to preserve what His people have been commissioned to safeguard. The scriptures are replete with examples in which divine truth was lost, corrupted, or neglected, not because God failed, but because His stewards did. The Restoration was itself necessitated by such apostasy.

One of the most striking biblical examples of this dynamic is found in the account of King Josiah's reforms. In 2 Kings 22, during temple renovations in the seventh century BCE, the high priest Hilkiah discovered "the book of the law"—most scholars interpret this as an early form of Deuteronomy—that had been lost or forgotten for generations. When it was read aloud to Josiah, he tore his garments in grief, realizing that Israel had been living in deep violation of God's commandments. The discovery prompted sweeping national repentance, covenant renewal, and reformation. But the tragedy lies in the premise— how could such a central text have been lost in the very house of the Lord?

The loss of scripture within a covenant community is not a theoretical danger. It has happened. And it happened not in Babylon or Egypt, but in the temple precincts of Jerusalem, among the priests, the rulers, and the chosen people.

The Book of Mormon reinforces this pattern. The people of Zarahemla, identified as descendants of Mulek, are explicitly described as having lost their scriptural records and, as a consequence, their cultural memory, religious identity, and linguistic clarity (Omni 1:17). Mosiah's discovery of these people, and the subsequent teaching of the Nephite language and gospel to them, serves as a sobering cautionary tale that when scripture is lost, identity collapses, and apostasy sets in silently but swiftly.

Apostasy, then, is not something that occurs only "out there." It is not reserved for secular society or hostile nations. It occurs within the house of Israel. To assume that because the priesthood remains on the earth, we are somehow immune from communal spiritual decline is, at best, naive, and at worst, spiritually arrogant. The priesthood authority may indeed remain unrevoked in this final dispensation, but the fruits of that priesthood (doctrinal clarity, revelatory power, scriptural fidelity, etc.) are not guaranteed without active stewardship.

The Book of Mormon illustrates that priesthood legitimacy does not automatically equate to righteousness. For one example, the textual and historical breadcrumbs suggest that the priests of King Noah may have originally inherited legitimate priesthood authority through the line of Nephite kings and religious offices. Yet even with that authority, they distorted the scriptures, justified sin, and ultimately led a generation into apostasy (Mosiah 11–17). Their descent was not due to external persecution or theological assault from outsiders, but due to internal corruption, complacency, and scriptural ignorance.

This is the warning we must heed. The covenant community is always at risk of forgetting its charge, not through overt rebellion, but through a "dwindling." When scriptural study is reduced, when doctrinal depth is traded for sentimentality, and when spiritual stewardship is presumed rather than practiced, apostasy does not erupt. It simply seeps in.

To suggest that the Lord would unilaterally prevent such a decline is to abdicate responsibility under the guise of faith. God does not forcibly preserve what He has asked His people to protect. If we do not cherish the word, we risk repeating the sorrowful pattern of Josiah's generation—rediscovering, too late, what was once entrusted to our care.

It is significant that within the sacred context of the modern temple endowment, arguably the most theologically concentrated and symbolically rich ordinance in contemporary Latter-day Saint practice, participants covenant to uphold the law of the gospel as found in the holy scriptures and are specifically charged to avoid "lightmindedness." This term, while rarely defined in contemporary discourse, carries considerable spiritual weight. It suggests a disposition of casualness toward sacred things, a failure to appreciate the gravity of covenantal truth, and a tendency to substitute ease for earnestness.

In this light, the widespread simplification of gospel instruction and curriculum in recent decades deserves careful scrutiny. The Correlation movement brought undeniable administrative benefits and enabled the global Church to operate with a shared instructional foundation. However, as with any institutional reform, its fruits have included both gains and losses.

One unintended consequence of Correlation, especially as carried forward into the Come, Follow Me era, has been a form of cultural over-homogenization. Gospel discussions, lesson materials, and even testimonies have increasingly gravitated toward emotionally affirming and intellectually unchallenging patterns. Over time, this has cultivated not only theological passivity, but a kind of performative orthodoxy—Saints say the "right" things and feel the "right" emotions, but often struggle to articulate scriptural doctrines, engage with complexity, or sustain a testimony under the pressure of contradiction, nuance, or adversity.

This condition is not merely cultural, but spiritual. Lightmindedness, in a modern context, may not take the form of open mockery or casual irreverence. It may instead appear as chronic superficiality, where the things of God are regularly spoken of, but rarely wrestled with. When difficult doctrines are sidestepped, when sacred texts are cherry-picked for slogans, and when gospel teaching becomes a parade of platitudes rather than a feast of truth, the soul is left undernourished, even if outward participation remains high.

The temple's inclusion of lightmindedness as a spiritual danger is thus not peripheral, but prophetic. In covenantal worship, God signals that the manner in which we engage with His word matters. When we reduce the gospel to sentiment, when we flatten its narrative into cheerful generalities, we risk more than boredom—we risk estrangement from the revelatory power that scripture is meant to mediate.

The Church of Jesus Christ of Latter-day Saints is a covenant people, entrusted with divine truth. But that stewardship comes with expectation. And the warning embedded in the temple is not purely symbolic. If we treat divine things lightly—if we are content with a culture that prizes correlation over contemplation—we may find that the light we claim to carry is dimming. The covenantal charge is not to preserve familiarity, but to seek depth, reverence, and the transformative power of God's word.

The ongoing decline of scriptural literacy within the Church of Jesus Christ of Latter-day Saints presents a growing concern whose consequences, though not entirely predictable, fall within a historically recognizable spectrum. It is impossible to say with precision how this trend will ultimately unfold. In the best-case scenario, the present crisis could serve as a catalyst for a spiritual awakening or doctrinal reformation, what might be described as a "corrective" movement that calls the Saints back to the scriptures with renewed fervor and covenantal integrity. A middle-ground possibility, perhaps the one most visible in the present moment, is prolonged institutional stagnation—a slow drift toward cultural and theological irrelevance, where core doctrines are retained in name but no longer animated by lived conviction or scriptural depth.

However, the worst-case scenario, and the one that appears most consistent with historical precedent, is that a continued departure from scriptural engagement will lead to widespread disaffection, doctrinal confusion, and internal fracture. History demonstrates with striking consistency that when institutions—religious, philosophical, or political—lose connection to their foundational identities, a collapse or transformation typically follows within three to five generations. Importantly, the initial signs are almost never public crises. They manifest first as internal erosion.

The scriptures themselves are filled with such warnings. Prophets in the Book of Mormon consistently exhort their people to "remember, remember," precisely because forgetting—especially forgetting God's word—leads rapidly to apostasy and collapse. This pattern plays out repeatedly in the historical record:

- In ancient Israel, the discovery of the lost book of the law during the reign of Josiah initiated a short-lived spiritual revival, but this was not enough to halt the nation's downward trajectory. Within a century, the kingdom fell to Babylon.

- The transition from Second Temple Judaism to Rabbinic Judaism took little more than 150 years following the Roman destruction of the temple in 70 CE. That transformation arose from internal spiritual fragmentation as much as it did from external pressure.

- The Great Apostasy, as understood in Restoration thought, began not centuries but decades after the ascension of Christ and death of the apostles. As apostolic authority was lost and scripture neglected, the early Church drifted toward creeds and councils, replacing covenant with hierarchy.

- Even our Restoration cousins in the Community of Christ (formerly RLDS) offer a sobering example—within 80 years of foundational doctrinal detachment from the Book of Mormon, the denomination underwent a theological realignment so extensive that it now identifies with progressive Protestant Christianity more than with Restoration theology.

- The Protestant Reformation itself, sparked by Martin Luther's 95 Theses in 1517, gave way to doctrinal fragmentation within about 3–4 generations, as *sola scriptura* ideals were interpreted in increasingly divergent ways without a unifying interpretive tradition.

These patterns consistently affirm that a community's theological memory is never self-sustaining. It must be preserved through deliberate engagement with scripture, active teaching, and covenant renewal. When this is neglected, the outcome is relatively predictable.

What follows in this chapter is a forecast—not a prophecy, but a reasoned projection—grounded in the warning signs explored in depth in Chapter 3. Whereas Chapter 3 outlined the general process of spiritual starvation, this chapter will examine the plausible outcomes that may be expected to emerge as a result of that condition. I will probably not live to witness the culmination of these trends, but I am persuaded that the groundwork is already being laid, as evidenced by the observable symptoms previously discussed. Unless meaningfully reversed, many of these outcomes could reach full expression by the eve of the 22nd century.

I have arranged the following scenarios in a likely chronological progression, from short-term consequences that may unfold within a generation, to long-term structural transformations that could reshape the Church's identity entirely. These projections are shared not with fatalism, but with hope that identifying the trajectory may encourage reform. I invite the reader to receive what follows as a prayerfully offered warning, rooted in historical pattern and scriptural insight.

The Loss of Communal Scriptural Culture

We could reasonably expect to see a complete privatization of gospel learning. Teaching and study would come to be seen primarily as personal responsibilities or optional devotions, rather than as sacred communal duties. The decline of a communal scriptural culture in favor of self-paced reading and sporadic, optional discussion would represent a shift in the practice of discipleship itself. If this trajectory is left unchecked, the long-term result would be a Church in which members are sacramentally bound but intellectually and doctrinally disconnected— each carrying the covenant individually, but no longer interpreting, remembering, or embodying it together. In such a climate, this loss of scriptural fluency would mark a generational unraveling of the faith's foundation.

The Loss of Teaching as a Spiritual Gift

We could reasonably expect to see teaching no longer recognized as a divinely endowed spiritual gift. Teaching within the Church would devolve into a logistical necessity assigned by rotation. Teaching is a sacred gift given by God for the edification of the Saints, contingent on faith, preparation, and alignment with the Spirit. In earlier periods of Church history, teaching was often viewed with deep reverence. The teacher was not simply a facilitator of conversation or an organizer of group dialogue, but a witness of doctrine, one whose calling was to illuminate gospel truth with clarity and conviction. In a climate of widespread scriptural illiteracy, that vision would fade. Over time, the Saints would begin to treat teaching as something anyone could do at any time, regardless of preparation, spiritual maturity, or doctrinal literacy.

Collapse of Ministerial Competency at the Local Level

We could reasonably expect to see a collapse of ministerial competency at the local level. This would occur as ecclesiastical leadership roles are increasingly filled by well-intentioned individuals who lack the doctrinal fluency, scriptural familiarity, and theological depth required to truly shepherd a covenant people. In such a scenario, Elders Quorum and Relief Society presidencies, Bishoprics, and even stake leadership would find themselves proficient in administration and enthusiastic in fellowship, but insufficiently grounded in scripture to offer real spiritual nourishment. In time, what would emerge are spiritually "orphaned" wards—congregations where few, if any, could confidently articulate doctrine, answer complex questions, or teach with the clarity and conviction that comes from immersion in God's word.

Increased Dependency on Devotional Literature and Social Media

We could reasonably expect to see members experience a profound shift in the source and shape of their doctrinal engagement. The Standard Works would increasingly be supplemented, if not supplanted, by a steady diet of devotional literature and digital content. Scripture would not disappear outright, but it would lose its central authority in the lived religious experience of the Saints and be replaced by easily consumable materials designed more for emotional affirmation than for covenantal instruction.

We might expect to see Deseret Book bestsellers occupying prominent space within the doctrinal imagination of many Latter-day Saints, alongside the rise of LDS-themed social media influencers who wield considerable influence over the spiritual consumption habits of contemporary members. In essence, theological engagement would begin to be shaped less by sustained scriptural study and more by aesthetic appeal, viral relatability, and algorithmic reinforcement. As this shift deepens, spiritual reflection would essentially be reduced to soundbites and sentimentality, disconnected from the broader narrative and theological scaffolding of the Restoration. Over time, members may lose the ability to distinguish between inspired teachings and popular consensus.

Erosion of Scriptural Language

We could reasonably expect to see an erosion of scriptural language in prayer, teaching, and testimony. This would unfold as a quiet transformation in the spiritual cadence and vocabulary of worship, leading over time to a less reverent and less covenantally attuned religious culture. As members become less familiar with the scriptures, the language of Zion would begin to fade from the collective lexicon. In its place would arise a mode of expression shaped more by contemporary speech patterns and popular devotionalism. Public prayers would start to sound more casual, sacrament talks would increasingly rely on conversational tone, and testimonies would shift toward emotive reflections. Over time, this linguistic drift would result in a degradation of the spiritual texture of worship—a sort of softening of spiritual edges. When this happens, even the sacred will begin to sound quite ordinary.

The Reduction of the Gospel

We could reasonably expect to see a reduction of the gospel to a generic ethic of "niceness." In such a context, the richness and demands of covenantal discipleship would be supplanted by a superficial emphasis on being agreeable, avoiding discomfort, and cultivating a conflict-averse spirituality. Love would be framed primarily as affirmation, and righteousness reimagined as inoffensiveness. In public discourse, the Savior's teachings would be distilled into platitudes such as "be kind," "don't judge," and "just love everyone"—all valid in context, but stripped of their doctrinal and prophetic weight. The more difficult and confrontational aspects of Christ's ministry would be sidelined as exceptions, rationalized away as circumstantial, or ignored altogether. In time, doctrinal convictions would be seen as divisive, and even the call to repentance would be framed as "un-Christlike." This deformation of the gospel would not only affect how members behave but also how they perceive righteousness itself. The bar of discipleship would lower from covenantal faithfulness to social harmony.

Scripture as Symbol, Not Substance

We could reasonably expect to see a gradual transformation of scripture into a largely symbolic artifact. In such a condition, the scriptures may continue to be revered in form but neglected in function. They would be treated more as tokens of religious identity than as the living word of God. A key indicator of this shift would be the increasing reliance on out-of-context quotations and topical discussions in place of sustained scriptural study. As a result, scriptural phrases would become spiritually decorative, essentially used to endorse a mood or sentiment rather than to anchor teaching in revealed truth. In such a scenario, the tragedy is not that the scriptures are rejected, but that they are no longer needed.

Decreased Scriptural Echo in Blessings

We could reasonably expect to see revelatory experiences such as priesthood and patriarchal blessings gradually take on a more generic and therapeutic tone, reflecting the broader spiritual malnourishment of the community. In a culture where scripture is no longer a shared vernacular, even those called to sacred office may unintentionally begin to rely more heavily on generalized spiritual language than on revelatory symbolism grounded in scripture. This, of course, runs the risk of blessings becoming inspirational rather than instructional. The result is not false prophecy, but dulled prophecy—still sacred, but no longer sharp. Ultimately, if blessings lose their rootedness in scripture, they will lose

106

their power to connect the Saints to God's covenantal work throughout history, including their place within the unfolding redemptive story that began with Israel and culminates in Christ.

The Diminishment of the Sacrament as Covenant Renewal

We could reasonably expect to see a diminishment of the sacrament as a covenantal ordinance. Over time, this sacred rite would be increasingly reduced to a symbolic gesture of inclusion or emotional uplift, rather than understood as a deliberate and recurring renewal of specific scriptural covenants. Without a grounding in the doctrinal texts that define the ordinance, members may begin to speak of the sacrament in increasingly vague or therapeutic terms, such as a time to "recharge," "feel peace," or "reset for the week." As this shift deepens, the language surrounding the sacrament would also degrade, losing its scriptural clarity. Testimonies and talks would begin to describe the sacrament less in terms of baptismal renewal or covenantal alignment, and more in terms of subjective experience of "feeling loved" or "feeling clean." Members would still gather, prayers would still be spoken, and emblems still passed, but the spiritual contract(s) being enacted would no longer be recognized or internalized.

Increasing Membership, Decreasing Discipleship

We could reasonably expect to see the emergence of a statistical paradox—the appearance of institutional strength measured by membership growth, even as actual discipleship deteriorates. In this scenario, the Church may continue to report significant increases in membership due to demographic and geographic factors, while simultaneously experiencing declining activity rates and general engagement across large swaths of the global body.

Several trends could contribute to this. First, birth rates among multigenerational Latter-day Saint families—particularly outside Western industrialized nations—will continue to generate natural growth in raw membership numbers. Second, the global expansion of the Church, particularly in parts of Africa, Southeast Asia, and Latin America, is likely to yield steady increases in conversions, bolstered by localized enthusiasm and missionary efforts. Third, institutional reporting structures that emphasize baptisms and membership records, rather than ongoing faithfulness and retention, will further reinforce a narrative of global vitality.

However, these numbers would obscure a much different spiritual reality. If scriptural literacy continues to decline within both the missionary force and the general membership, the result would be a growing body of baptized individuals who lack the doctrinal grounding necessary for enduring discipleship. By the mid- to late-21st century, the Church could well surpass 30 million members on paper, yet have fewer than 3 to 5 million actively participating worldwide—and potentially only 1 to 2 million who could reasonably demonstrate scriptural fluency. This would produce what may be termed a "Potemkin Church" effect—a spiritual institution that appears robust when measured externally, but in reality suffers from internal fragility, marked by diminishing gospel comprehension and shallow doctrinal commitment.

I believe this item, more than any other on the list, will prove to be the most lasting and catastrophic consequence for the Church.

An Age Inversion in Disaffiliation

We could reasonably expect to see a marked increase in disaffiliation among members in their 40s, 50s, and 60s, those who, in previous generations, would have been considered the stabilizing core of the Church. While much attention is currently given to youth and young adult inactivity, a more sobering trend may lie ahead—the gradual erosion of commitment among older, lifelong Latter-day Saints, many of whom may have remained active for decades more out of habit, culture, or expectation than true conversion or conviction.

This shift could be described as an "age inversion" in Church vitality. We could see some wards and branches led by a handful of earnest youth and young adults, while middle-aged members quietly disengage. For many in this demographic, disillusionment would be the driving force. After years, perhaps decades, of Church service, they may find themselves increasingly spiritually hungry, yet unsure why. Having been raised on sentiment and institutional loyalty rather than deep scriptural roots, they may feel as those who "have sown much, and bring in little" (Haggai 1:6). As trials accumulate or life slows down, these members may realize their spiritual foundation was more social than covenantal. Without rootedness in scripture, they begin to "wither" in the heat of adversity, as Christ warned in the parable of the sower (Matthew 13:5–6).

In practical terms, the consequences for this would be severe. A collapse of leadership depth would emerge. In many wards, the traditional reservoir of capable, mature priesthood holders and seasoned Relief Society leaders may vanish. Returned missionaries in their twenties may find themselves carrying the burdens of Elders Quorum presidencies or teaching gospel doctrine alone, as the generational structure inverts.

Some youth may, paradoxically, rise as spiritual dissenters from this lukewarm culture, seeking depth their parents never found. But broadly, this scenario anticipates a future in which Church activity skews younger in isolated pockets, while the once-reliable middle-aged base retreats into cultural identification without covenantal engagement. As Paul warned of the last days, there will be those who "have a form of godliness, but deny the power thereof" (2 Timothy 3:5). And as Moroni lamented, churches built up by pride in the latter days would be "polluted" and would deny the gifts of God (Mormon 8:36–39).

Loss of Symbolic Literacy

We could reasonably expect to see an erosion of symbolic literacy among the Saints. In such a scenario, members of the Church of Jesus Christ of Latter-day Saints would increasingly participate in sacred ordinances without the necessary framework to understand their covenantal origins or symbolic intent. Members may still participate in ordinances, but without recognizing them as part of a divinely revealed structure rooted in sacred texts. In this diminished condition, sacred symbols risk becoming cultural artifacts—respected perhaps, but no longer deeply understood. This phenomenon is already evident in our sacred temple signs, which were once presented alongside the signs of the penalties, now omitted from the endowment ceremony. Those who have received their endowments after 1990 are likely to view these signs as merely mysterious hand gestures, unaware of their deeper historical context and meaning.

As symbolic illiteracy deepens, confusion and/or indifference would arise. Ordinances could be seen as arbitrary, outdated, or even burdensome, stripped of their revelatory function and reduced to institutional markers. The ultimate consequence of this loss would be a crisis of theological identity. A covenant people who cannot read the symbols of their own faith become removed from their historical and doctrinal roots.

Fragmentation of Scriptural Interpretation

We could reasonably expect to see a fragmentation of scriptural interpretation across the body of the Church. Without a shared foundation of literacy in the Standard Works, scripture would increasingly be interpreted through individualized and relativistic lenses, giving rise to what might be termed interpretive pluralism or devotional subjectivism. The once-common language of covenantal exegesis and prophetic context would gradually dissolve into a mixture of personal impressions and isolated readings. This would probably be done in the name of "likening scripture," but the disintegration of interpretive unity would start to produce alarming recurrences of phrases like "that scripture means something different to everyone" or "that's just how I feel when I read this section." This interpretive drift would open the door to competing intra-church spiritualities, where individuals or even wards adopt subtly divergent theological emphases, moral outlooks, or eschatological assumptions. Scripture would become less a unifying voice and more a customizable resource.

The Rise of Tribalism Within the Church

We could reasonably expect to see a steady rise of tribalism within the Church through its internal fragmentation. In such a climate, members would remain institutionally affiliated while becoming increasingly doctrinally divergent, socially fragmented, and spiritually detached from the unifying canon of the Standard Works. This fragmentation would likely manifest in two broad directions. On one side, members may turn to alternative spiritual authorities—political ideologies, charismatic social media influencers, or culturally dominant narratives—to make sense of moral, social, and doctrinal questions. On the other side, members may drift toward what might be called parallel spiritual subcultures, loosely affiliated groups within the Church that reimagine what it means to be a Latter-day Saint. Though these groups may coexist within the same wards or stakes, they would increasingly operate with distinct spiritual grammars—their own vocabularies, social norms, and theological priorities. What would result is ecclesial dissonance—a Church that remains structurally unified while becoming theologically incoherent. Without scripture at the center, the Restoration risks becoming a contested platform for competing visions, rather than a revealed path toward Zion. Zion, after all, is defined not merely by institutional affiliation, but by being of one heart and one mind (Moses 7:18).

Muting of Prophetic Tension

We could reasonably expect to see a muting of prophetic tension within the collective imagination of the Saints. That is, the scriptural function of prophets as divine disruptors, moral agitators, and covenant enforcers would be gradually replaced by a far more comfortable and palatable model—the prophet as motivational speaker, institutional caretaker, or cultural ambassador. In such a model, prophets would be seen less as seers and revelators, and more as inspirational figures whose primary task is to uplift, reassure, and manage public perception. Calls to repentance may be received as discouraging or even unkind. Warnings may be dismissed as outdated or overly negative. And prophetic authority may be subconsciously evaluated according to how agreeable or affirming its messages feel.

A For-Profit Spiritual Industry of "LDS-Adjacent" Voices

We could reasonably expect to see the rise of a for-profit spiritual industry populated by LDS-adjacent voices. In the absence of doctrinal clarity and deep engagement with the Standard Works, members would increasingly turn to influencers, authors, podcasters, therapists, and content creators as primary sources of spiritual nourishment, emotional guidance, and theological interpretation. Over time, they may function as a kind of "soft clergy," individuals whose teachings are more widely shared, more attentively followed, and more deeply internalized than those found in official Church curriculum or General Conference addresses. Workshops, online courses, curated devotionals, and subscription-based coaching models would become normalized. While these platforms would probably avoid overt contradiction of Church teachings, they would often reframe, dilute, or sideline core doctrines through omission, reinterpretation, or selective emphasis. The long-term result would be a Church in which members appear active but are, in reality, being discipled by media ecosystems rather than by scripture or prophetic teaching. At some point within this shift, the Restoration itself risks being recast as just another lifestyle brand among many.

Rise of Post-Ordinance Church Participation Models

We could reasonably expect to see future generations of Latter-day Saints adopting frameworks of Church participation in which sacred ordinances such as baptism, endowment, and sealing are retained as symbolic milestones or cultural rites of passage, but are no longer understood or lived out as binding, ongoing covenants requiring active discipleship within the body of Christ. This shift would give rise to a growing subset of individuals who receive saving ordinances—perhaps for familial or

112

social reasons—but subsequently choose to live entirely outside the ecclesiastical and communal life of the Church. This trend may also be reflected in the evolution of temple presentation itself, where periodic adjustments to language and form risk being interpreted by members as a progressive dilution of covenantal seriousness. In such a context, the endowment could be perceived more as a meditative experience or symbolic empowerment than a rigorous initiation into priesthood responsibilities and divine law.

Temple Decline and Vacant Temple Buildings

We could reasonably expect to see the decline of temple attendance and the underutilization of sacred temple spaces. It would not be surprising to see a temple district encompassing tens of thousands of nominal members, yet only a few hundred recommend holders actively engaged in temple worship. Temples once filled with daily endowment sessions and youth proxy baptisms may be reduced to operating just a few days per week—or, in some districts, only a few days per month. Small temples in formerly robust stakes might find themselves nearly empty for long stretches of time. In developing areas where growth has slowed or plateaued, temples might stand as monuments of past momentum, visited only by traveling Church leaders, youth conferences, or the rare tour group. A temple can only thrive among a people who understand and prioritize the doctrines the temple enshrines—covenants, atonement, proxy redemption, eternal sealing, and divine priesthood order. Each of these core truths is richly taught in scripture. When scriptural knowledge diminishes, so too does temple literacy. Members may continue to attend out of habit or expectation, but if the ritual is divorced from its revelatory roots, the experience becomes shallow.

Artificial Prophets and Algorithmic Revelation

We could reasonably expect to see the emergence of AI-driven algorithmic systems that function as quasi-authoritative sources of doctrinal insight among members of the Church. This crisis would not stem from malicious intent, but from technological convenience. Large language models could be trained on the full corpus of the Standard Works, every General Conference address ever delivered, Church manuals, scholarly commentary, and even the stylistic cadence of prophets both ancient and modern. These systems would be capable of producing instantaneous responses to complex theological questions, offering synthesized doctrinal explanations, and generating tailored spiritual reflections. For members lacking a firm foundation in scripture, such tools would appear more reliable, consistent, or "spiritually clear" than human teachers, whose instruction inevitably varies in tone, preparation, and interpretive depth. Revelation would no longer be sought through divine mediation and covenantal stewardship, but through data synthesis divorced from spiritual authority and accountability. The prophetic mantle would not be explicitly denied, but subtly eclipsed—supplanted by a more responsive, personalized, and intellectually gratifying rival.

Increased Revelation That Is Not Canonized

We could reasonably expect to see the expansion of a body of non-canonized revelation that function practically as scripture in the devotional and doctrinal life of members. In such a scenario, the Church—responding to widespread spiritual disorientation and doctrinal drift—would increasingly issue prophetic guidance in the form of general epistles, apostolic declarations, conference talks with elevated doctrinal weight, or presidency-authored clarifications. Like *The Family: A Proclamation to the World* or the *Bicentennial Proclamation on the Restoration*, these texts would be received and treated as authoritative, often quoted in lessons and referenced in policy, despite lacking the formal status of canon.

This development would arise, in part, from the institutional Church's increasing hesitancy to canonize new material, an understandable response to its global diversity and heightened sensitivities surrounding doctrinal rigidity. However, this caution would inadvertently blur the boundary between prophetic counsel and revealed doctrine. As a result, interpretive unity risks fragmentation. Some members may come to anchor their doctrinal worldview almost exclusively in recent statements or initiatives, while others may question their permanence or revelatory status, particularly when such language appears policy-oriented or temporally constrained. Over time, this tension could erode confidence in what "counts" as doctrine, introducing ambiguity into the theological core of the Church and destabilizing doctrinal coherence.

Loss of Prophetic Vision

We could reasonably expect to see the gradual loss of prophetic vision. This is not to say there will be a cessation of prophetic leadership, but a profound diminishment in the Church's collective understanding of what prophetic communion with God entails. Over time, this would not only dilute the doctrinal framework that sustains prophetic authority, but also sever the Church from the essence of the Restoration itself. Members may come to see modern revelation as administrative guidance rather than divine communion. The prophetic office may still be respected institutionally, but its charismatic and revelatory character could fade from memory or be reinterpreted through reductionist assumptions. Instead of expecting living prophets to literally converse with God, future generations may come to believe that such communion is figurative, mystical, or metaphorical, such as impressions through prayer rather than a face-to-face encounter. This theological drift would effectively transform the prophet from a seer and revelator into a spiritual administrator, trusted for his wisdom but no longer expected to speak with divine voice.

Diminished Capacity for Zion Building

We could reasonably expect to see a diminished capacity for Zion-building within the Church. The concept of Zion would gradually devolve into a vague ideal—community harmony, moral uplift, or cultural cohesion—untethered from its covenantal demands and eschatological trajectory. In such a context, members would increasingly conflate Zion-building with sociological community-building—the promotion of kindness, inclusivity, and emotional wellness. The term *Zion* would likely persist in Church discourse, but its scriptural depth and prophetic urgency could be reduced to metaphor, divorced from the concrete, covenantal vision revealed through modern prophets and canonized texts. In this way, the theological richness of Zion risks being supplanted by cultural sentimentality.

This confusion may be further compounded by the enduring ambiguity surrounding the Independence, Missouri temple lot, a site identified by revelation as the center place of the New Jerusalem (D&C 57:1–3). In the absence of visible progress toward its acquisition or development, future generations may quietly relinquish belief in its literal fulfillment, reinterpreting such prophecies as symbolic, deferred, or obsolete. Conversely, should the Church acquire the temple lot or incorporate the existing Community of Christ temple into Latter-day Saint temple worship, such an act could catalyze doctrinal renewal and reawaken the collective imagination surrounding Zion's fulfillment.

But without that renewed vision, and without the scriptural literacy required to sustain it, Zion risks becoming a relic of Restoration rhetoric rather than an anticipatory project of a covenant people. The Saints cannot build what they no longer recognize, and they cannot recognize what they no longer read.

Remnant Zion or Institutional Rebranding

We could reasonably expect to see the Church of Jesus Christ of Latter-day Saints facing an existential crossroads—one that demands either a covenantal resurgence among a scripturally literate remnant or a gradual transition into institutional rebranding that preserves outward form while diluting inner function.

The first path envisions a smaller yet spiritually vigorous body of Saints—individuals who maintain fidelity to the covenants, doctrines, and mission of the Restoration. This remnant, though perhaps numerically modest, would remain doctrinally anchored, scripturally fluent, and prophetically aligned. It would preserve the vision of Zion as a covenant-based society prepared to receive the Lord at his coming. In such a scenario, institutional structures would endure, but the true spiritual vitality would emerge from a consecrated core of disciples who have not forgotten the divine mandate to gather Israel, build Zion, and prepare the earth for millennial transformation.

The second and far more probable path is one of institutional rebranding. In this trajectory, the Church may continue to grow numerically and expand globally, but its emphasis would gradually shift toward community cohesion, interfaith engagement, and humanitarian outreach, often at the expense of covenantal distinctiveness. Doctrinal instruction would become increasingly generalized, prophetic expectation would be softened, and uniquely Restorationist claims would be downplayed in favor of broader, more socially palatable religious values. The result would be a religious institution that is outwardly indistinguishable from many other Christian denominations.

Selective Persecution of Scripturally Literate Saints

We could reasonably expect to see a selective persecution of scripturally faithful Saints via social, cultural, and intra-ecclesiastical marginalization. As scriptural engagement declines and doctrinal conviction is increasingly viewed as socially or emotionally abrasive, those who continue to anchor their discipleship in scripture and covenant would find themselves viewed not as exemplary, but as disruptive. Such individuals would not likely be excommunicated or officially condemned. Rather, they would be dismissed through soft exclusion—removed from teaching callings for being "too intense," passed over in councils for being "out of step," or gently rebuked for lacking so-called orthodoxy. Their public loyalty to the Standard Works, particularly when it challenges cultural accommodation or doctrinal relativism, will be interpreted as rigidity, pride, or even dissent.

This trend would probably extend beyond ecclesiastical circles. Those who remain openly aligned with the scriptures may also face legal or professional consequences, especially in regions where freedom of belief is subordinated to ideological conformity. Thus, persecution in the last days may take the quieter form of exclusion, isolation, and dismissal of the faithful as socially unfit or spiritually obsolete.

Ideological Schism Without Organizational Split

We could reasonably expect to see a growing internal polarization resembling a schism without resulting in an actual organizational split. In such a scenario, the structural integrity of the Church would remain outwardly intact, but its doctrinal cohesion would begin to fracture along ideological lines. While emerging groups would remain institutionally loyal, their underlying assumptions about the nature of the gospel, the purpose of the Church, and the role of prophetic authority would begin to diverge in increasingly incompatible ways. What would emerge is a geographic and cultural patchwork—regions where gospel instruction retains doctrinal depth and clarity coexisting with areas where lessons become functionally doctrineless. A single ward may persist in form and governance, but it would increasingly house multiple theologies— distinct, and in some cases, mutually unintelligible. Over time, this divergence would erode mutual understanding to such a degree that Saints lose the ability to speak the same spiritual language, even while remaining under the same institutional roof.

The Largest Church Split Since the RLDS Tradition

We could reasonably expect to see the largest ecclesiastical rupture within the Church of Jesus Christ of Latter-day Saints since the schism that followed the death of Joseph Smith in 1844. While contemporary members may find such a possibility unthinkable, historical and doctrinal patterns suggest that sustained erosion of scriptural engagement can and does eventually precipitate institutional fragmentation. When scriptural norms are displaced by culturally adaptive teachings, devotional rhetoric, or therapeutic theology, a vacuum emerges—one that invites conflicting

118

worldviews to arise and take root within the same ecclesial structure. Over time, without a clear scriptural anchor, what counts as "doctrine" becomes entirely relative, and members increasingly define orthodoxy by consensus or culture. Such a condition is structurally unsustainable.

Should this trajectory continue, the possibility of a formal rupture within the institutional Church becomes increasingly likely. Although such a fracture would certainly not require an internal leadership crisis, it would almost certainly be exacerbated by the public excommunication or defection of one or more high-ranking general authorities. Historically, such events were not uncommon. Between 1838 and 1905, apostles were excommunicated or removed with some regularity, with the longest interval between such incidents being only 24 years. Another excommunication occurred in 1943. Since then, no apostle has been excommunicated, marking an unprecedented 80+ year gap—a full three generations. While this might be interpreted as a sign of sustained leadership unity and fidelity, it also means that the modern Church is profoundly unaccustomed to institutional dissent at the highest levels. The excommunication of an apostle today, particularly on charges of apostasy or doctrinal divergence, would likely spark unprecedented polarization. Given the Church's global scale, the instantaneous spread of information, and a membership base increasingly divided along cultural and ideological lines, such an event would not only dominate public discourse but could become the symbolic catalyst for a broader schism.

Chapter 6: The Iron Rod

Lehi's vision of the Tree of Life, recorded in 1 Nephi 8 and further expanded in 1 Nephi 11–15, offers what may be the most enduring spiritual metaphor in all of Restoration scripture. It is a sweeping narrative of covenantal choice, filled with striking symbols—a tree whose fruit is "desirable above all," an iron rod, a mist of darkness, and a great and spacious building filled with mockers. Each represents an archetype of discipleship or its antithesis. But amid all these symbols, it is the iron rod that determines the outcome.

Much attention is often given to the great and spacious building—and for good reason. It is an image of collective pride, intellectual vanity, and performative religiosity. It is described as "filled with people, both old and young, both male and female," adorned in fine clothing, and united in mocking those who seek to partake of the fruit of the tree. They represent the pride of the world, the spiritually self-assured who never intended to walk the covenant path. As Joseph Smith would later explain, those in the building are consigned to mediocrity through ridicule and apathy. They are not wrestling with faith. They are simply amused by it. They never set foot on the path and were never holding the iron rod.

But for all the power of that image, it is not the most tragic figure in Lehi's vision. That role belongs to those who once held the iron rod and let it go.

The rod, Nephi explains, is the word of God (1 Nephi 11:25). It is the rod that leads directly to the tree, and it is the rod that must be grasped—continually, not casually—to withstand the mists of darkness, which symbolize the confusion, temptations, and distortions of a fallen world. Many in the vision fall away not because they hate the fruit or because they join the great and spacious building, but because they lose their grip on the rod. The mist overtakes them, and they are lost. The most devastating outcome in the entire vision is not rebellion, but disorientation. These are the people who once had the word of God in their hands and let it slip away.

That, I fear, is the Church I have come to know in many places. Not a church full of rebels, nor one openly antagonistic to faith, but a church unmoored from the iron rod. A people who once revered the word of God, but now—amid culture, comfort, and distraction—have replaced it with platitudes, programs, and sentiment.

We are witnessing a quiet migration, not always toward the great and spacious building, but away from the rod. And that distinction matters. Remember—those in the building never intended to walk the path. But those who let go of the rod once did. They may still attend meetings, speak in familiar tones, and perform outward duties, but without the rod, they are spiritually drifting, vulnerable to every mist of darkness that rises.

Unless we return—individually and collectively—to a disciplined, covenantal, daily holding of the word of God, we too will find ourselves lost. We will think we are still walking the path, when in fact we have been wandering in darkness with the rod somewhere behind us. Lehi and Nephi saw this. Joseph Smith warned of this. The Book of Mormon was given to prevent this.

Let us then return not merely to the memory of the scriptures, but to the actual grasping of them. Let us teach and live by the rod. Because the truth is painfully clear—we do not need to leave the Church to be lost. We only need to let go of the word of God.

When considering Lehi's vision of the iron rod and other prophetic declarations concerning the latter-day Gentile church, it may be too limited a reading to conclude that the modern Church is simply failing to live up to divine expectations. A more compelling—and perhaps more sobering—interpretation is that we are not merely falling short of prophecy, but *fulfilling* it. In other words, the present condition of the

Church may not represent an unexpected deviation from the plan, but rather the very trajectory foreseen by ancient prophets.

This perspective calls to mind the warnings recorded in 2 Nephi regarding apostasy in the last days. These warnings were not directed at the world at large, but at those within Zion itself—"And others will [the devil] pacify, and lull them away into carnal security, that they will say: All is well in Zion; yea, Zion prospereth, all is well—and thus the devil cheateth their souls, and leadeth them away carefully down to hell... Therefore, wo be unto him that is at ease in Zion!" (2 Nephi 28:21, 24).

Moroni, writing in prophetic hindsight, expressed deep concern about the pride, materialism, and unbelief he foresaw among the people who would receive his record—"Why have ye polluted the holy church of God?...Why do ye adorn yourselves with that which hath no life...and suffer the hungry, and the needy, and the naked to pass by you, and notice them not?" (Mormon 8:36–39). His warning does not appear to be aimed at a world that rejects the Church, but rather a Church that forgets its own sacred purpose.

The Apostle Paul foresaw a time when those professing faith would not endure sound doctrine, but would heap to themselves teachers who would say "smooth things" (2 Timothy 4:3; cf. Isaiah 30:10). These prophecies are not external—they are internal. They describe conditions *within* the covenant community in the last days. In other words, the spiritual fatigue, doctrinal shallowness, and cultural dilution observable today are not really anomalies—they are fulfillments.

So then, the question must be asked—What does one do when they find themselves not merely observing prophecy, but living in the very midst of it? If we accept the premise that the modern Church may be fulfilling these scriptural warnings, the task is not merely to critique or lament, but to awaken. The prophets did not record these warnings for resignation, but for repentance. If the arc of history is bending toward apostasy or spiritual mediocrity, it becomes the solemn duty of the Saints—not to despair—but to rise, to remember, and to rebuild.

123

What, then, can be done? The solution is not merely better manuals or revised curricula, but a wholesale re-centering of scripture. The scriptures must again become the living core of all gospel instruction and discipleship, not just quoted occasionally in talks, but studied, taught, wrestled with, internalized, and lived. We must move beyond surface-level engagement and reclaim the scriptures as a covenantal language—a divine lexicon by which the Saints interpret their world, shape their character, and speak truth with power. If the Church is to preserve doctrinal depth, prophetic clarity, and spiritual vitality in the generations ahead, then the word must take primacy over personality, and doctrine over sentiment.

Only when the words of Christ, ancient prophets, and modern revelations become familiar upon the tongues and in the minds of the Saints will the community begin to speak with the voice of Zion. This means reclaiming a mode of expression that is shaped not by cultural cliché or therapeutic self-expression, but by scriptural cadence, covenantal clarity, and revelatory precision. The sentimental substitutions of the world—however well-intentioned—cannot substitute for the power of the word when it is rightly divided and spiritually taught.

What follows is a collection of ideas and proposals that have taken shape in my mind over the past several months. They are offered as suggestions for consideration, refinement, or even prayerful disagreement. I am just one member among millions. I do not claim prophetic insight. I am acutely aware that some of these ideas may never be implemented, whether due to practical constraints, cultural inertia, or institutional complexity. Still, if even a handful were seriously attempted, I believe they could help reverse—or at least slow—the spiritual consequences explored in the previous chapter. It is my hope that this chapter can serve as a starting point for broader conversations about how we, as a covenant people, might more fully return to the word and preserve the doctrinal inheritance entrusted to us.

Release a Churchwide Call to Repentance

The first and most urgent remedy must be spiritual in nature. The Church could consider issuing a formal, prophetic call to repentance concerning the widespread neglect of scripture across its membership. Such a call would not be unprecedented. Prophetic invitations to return to foundational commandments—such as Sabbath observance, chastity, or family worship—have long served as catalytic moments of reform within the Latter-day Saint tradition. A call of this kind would invite members to mourn the loss of doctrinal fluency, to fast for renewed spiritual hunger, and to recommit themselves to regular, substantive engagement with the Standard Works. In an age of distraction and spiritual superficiality, such a summons could signal a solemn re-centering of discipleship around the revealed word of God. More than just a cultural correction, this would be a covenantal realignment that reorients the Saints toward feasting upon the word as an act of worship, memory, and preparation for Zion.

Reemphasize the Standard Works as Superior to All Other Sources

In order to correct doctrinal drift and restore interpretive clarity, Church leadership could consider publicly reaffirming the primacy of the Standard Works as the ultimate scriptural authority in the restored gospel. While the teachings of modern prophets and apostles are indispensable, they are intended to expound and apply revealed scripture—not to replace or eclipse it. A growing trend among some members is to treat General Conference talks as primary sources of doctrine while relegating scripture to a supporting or decorative role. This inversion is not doctrinally sound. In every dispensation, canonized scripture has served as the standard by which prophetic counsel is measured and interpreted. Reestablishing this principle would ensure that Conference messages are understood within the enduring covenantal framework of the scriptures, not outside of it. A clear and public affirmation from the First Presidency could help re-anchor the Church's teaching culture in its revealed foundation, safeguarding against the sentimentality, misquotation, and selective proof-texting that often arise in the absence of a governing scriptural lens.

Elevate Scripture in General Conference

A vital step toward restoring doctrinal depth in the Church could be to intentionally elevate the role of scripture in General Conference addresses. While current talks often include scriptural references, these citations are frequently brief, symbolic, or supplementary—used to frame a larger narrative rather than to anchor it. By contrast, in earlier periods of Church history, leaders commonly read substantial passages from the Standard Works and then offered sustained exposition, often using the talk itself as a form of interpretive commentary. A return to that model would help reinforce the principle that modern revelation builds upon— not bypasses—ancient scripture. Talks could aim not only to inspire, but to instruct; not only to uplift, but to expound (see 3 Nephi 23:6). The Saints need to see how scripture functions in real-time doctrinal reasoning, modeled from the highest pulpits of the Church. Leaders who unpack verses, trace typologies, or explain prophetic patterns demonstrate not only personal scriptural fluency, but also invite the membership to reengage with the Standard Works as living texts. This approach would reestablish General Conference as a venue of rich, covenantal teaching, where the word of God is revealed anew through prophetic explanation.

Publish a Church-Approved Commentary on the Standard Works

To support doctrinal consistency and deepen scriptural engagement across the global Church, leaders could consider commissioning and publishing an official, Church-approved commentary on the Standard Works. Such a resource could offer historical context, theological insights, cross-references, and interpretive guidance to assist lay teachers, families, and students. While not intended to replace personal revelation or inspired teaching, this commentary could serve as a doctrinal scaffold for those seeking clarity and depth beyond the basic curriculum. In a

Church built upon lay instruction, a standardized commentary would help mitigate the increasing fragmentation of interpretation and support the cultivation of scriptural fluency across all demographics. It could also serve as a safeguard against both proof-texting and speculative doctrinal claims. Just as Elder James E. Talmage's writings once provided generations of Latter-day Saints with accessible but rigorous doctrinal tools, so too could a 21st-century equivalent help restore confidence in scripture as a living foundation.

Revamp or Replace the Current *Come, Follow Me* Curriculum

The Come, Follow Me curriculum could be critically re-evaluated in light of its pedagogical limitations. Its intentionally minimalistic and principle-focused design leaves many mature learners and teachers doctrinally undernourished. To better serve the diverse spiritual appetites of a global Church, a bifurcated approach could be considered—a general participatory track, ideal for families and new members, and a parallel expository track designed for more experienced learners and teachers seeking deeper engagement with scripture. The latter would include historical context, doctrinal exposition, cross-referencing among the Standard Works, and theological framing akin to former Gospel Doctrine manuals or institute-level instruction. Without such reform, the Church risks cultivating a generation of Saints whose spiritual diet is devotional but not doctrinal, familiar with gospel language but unacquainted with gospel substance. A multi-tiered curriculum would allow for both accessibility and depth, meeting members where they are while lifting them toward greater scriptural fluency, interpretive skill, and covenantal understanding.

Create an Official "Teacher's Book of Scripture"

To enhance the quality and consistency of lay instruction across the Church, leaders could consider an official *Teacher's Book of Scripture* be developed and distributed. This resource would serve as a doctrinally grounded, pedagogically useful reference volume—distinct from lesson manuals—designed specifically to support teachers, speakers, and study group facilitators in their preparation. It would include curated cross-references across the Standard Works, brief historical and cultural background notes, concise doctrinal commentary drawn from authoritative sources, and recommended teaching approaches for selected passages. This could function as a scaffolding aid to foster greater confidence and competence in scripture-based teaching. In a Church where instruction is largely entrusted to non-specialists, such a volume could play a critical role in bridging the gap between devotional familiarity and theological literacy. Like a simplified synthesis of institute manuals, doctrinal topics guides, and topical indexes, a *Teacher's Book of Scripture* would be an invaluable tool in promoting interpretive clarity, scriptural coherence, and reverence for the word of God.

Canonize Scriptural Teaching Standards for Ordinances

To safeguard the integrity and transformative power of sacred ordinances, the Church could consider formally codifying scriptural teaching standards for all covenantal preparation. While the administration of ordinances—such as baptism, confirmation, priesthood ordination, and temple rites—is conducted under priesthood authority, the doctrinal foundation for receiving these ordinances is often uneven and varies widely by local instruction. A canonized, scripture-based framework would ensure that candidates understand not merely the procedural aspects of ordinances, but their covenantal significance, doctrinal origins, and eternal trajectory. Instruction would be rooted in the scriptures themselves, drawing explicitly from texts such as Mosiah 18, 2 Nephi 31, D&C 84, and others that define the nature of discipleship and covenantal belonging. Such a move would not only elevate the theological clarity of Church instruction but also reinforce the sacredness of the ordinances by anchoring them in revealed language. Canonizing such standards—either through formal handbook revisions or a unified preparatory curriculum—would help ensure that those who make and renew covenants do so with "real intent" (Moroni 10:4), informed by the word of God rather than cultural assumption or superficial familiarity.

Train Clergy and Teachers in Theological Education

Given the increasingly complex spiritual needs of a global Church, ecclesiastical leaders must be not only administratively capable but also theologically informed. A formal initiative to provide theological education for bishops, stake presidents, temple presidents, and mission presidents could significantly elevate the doctrinal fluency of the Church's leadership corps. This could take the form of modular coursework—offered through BYU, Ensign College, or a centralized Church platform—focusing on scriptural exegesis, Restoration theology, covenantal history, and key doctrinal themes. These resources would be designed to be accessible yet rigorous, combining video instruction, readings, and periodic assessments to ensure retention and application. In tandem, doctrinal evaluation interviews could be instituted periodically at the stake level to assess leaders' ability to teach and apply core doctrines effectively. Such a program would not undermine spiritual gifts or revelation, but rather equip leaders to magnify those gifts with greater precision, confidence, and scriptural depth. As the Church grows in complexity and diversity, the ability of local and regional leaders to "expound all scriptures" (3 Nephi 23:6) will be critical to sustaining doctrinal unity and nourishing the Saints.

Reclaim the Expectation that Leaders Are Scripturally Fluent

In a Church governed by lay leadership, spiritual maturity must be matched by scriptural fluency. It is no longer sufficient for any organizational leaders to be merely administratively competent or well-intentioned. They must be doctrinally literate and capable of expounding the scriptures with clarity and conviction. Historically, Church leaders— especially in the early Restoration—were expected to be "mighty in the scriptures" (cf. Acts 18:24), able to teach correct principles from the revealed word of God. Reclaiming this expectation could mean treating scriptural understanding as a legitimate and essential qualification for ecclesiastical leadership, alongside spiritual discernment and moral integrity. Stake presidencies and Bishoprics might regularly assess the doctrinal readiness of potential leaders, not to create elitism, but to ensure that those entrusted with shepherding the flock are equipped to do so in the language and logic of the covenants. As scriptural illiteracy increases, so too does the risk of gospel distortion. By reaffirming scripture fluency as a leadership expectation, the Church can protect the theological integrity of its local units and re-anchor its ministries in the revealed foundations of the Restoration.

All Sacrament Talks and Lessons Reviewed by the Bishopric

To preserve doctrinal integrity and promote spiritual edification, ward Bishoprics could consider proactively reviewing all sacrament meeting talks and second-hour lesson plans in advance—not as a mechanism of censorship or control, but as an act of spiritual stewardship. In a lay-led church, the diversity of teaching backgrounds and theological assumptions can lead to wide variation in scriptural usage, doctrinal clarity, and pedagogical focus. A review process offers a safeguard against the inadvertent spread of speculative or incorrect doctrine, ensures alignment with the Church's scriptural and prophetic foundation, and fosters higher-quality instruction. This review would also serve as an opportunity for mentorship, enabling leaders to encourage richer scriptural exposition, reinforce the centrality of Christ, and guide teachers or speakers away from overreliance on anecdotes or sentimentality. Rather than discouraging participation, such a process affirms the sacredness of teaching and speaking in the name of the Lord (D&C 42:12–16). Just as priesthood ordinances are performed with care and preparation, so too should the delivery of doctrine in public settings be approached with reverence, thoughtfulness, and ecclesiastical oversight.

Require Scripture Citations in Every Sacrament Talk and Lesson

To reinforce the centrality of revealed truth in Latter-day Saint worship and instruction, sacrament meeting talks and second-hour lessons could be expected to include direct engagement with the scriptures. A talk or lesson that omits scriptural citation risks reducing gospel instruction to personal reflection or cultural sentiment, thereby severing it from its revelatory foundation. This expectation need not be enforced with rigidity, but should be gently and consistently modeled, taught, and, when necessary, corrected. Just as ordinances are performed using prescribed language and sacred structure, so too should public teaching be anchored in the word of God. Leaders can support this standard by regularly reminding speakers and teachers of their sacred responsibility to teach "out of the best books" (D&C 88:118), which first and foremost includes the Standard Works. Over time, normalizing this expectation would help shift the cultural tone of meetings and ensure that members are being fed by the scriptures themselves rather than merely the impressions or personalities of those presenting. Such a practice reaffirms that all Church teaching, at every level, must be grounded in "the law and the testimony" (Isaiah 8:20).

Reinstitute Teacher Interviews and Development Meetings

To elevate the quality and doctrinal soundness of gospel instruction, wards and stakes could consider reinstituting regular teacher interviews and structured teacher development meetings. These meetings—once a normative aspect of Church practice—can provide mentorship, textual training, and space for reflective dialogue on teaching and doctrine. Rather than merely reviewing classroom logistics, these gatherings would center on deepening scriptural fluency, improving teaching methods, and fostering spiritual preparation. In a lay-led church, teachers vary widely in their backgrounds and confidence with the scriptures. Ongoing development is essential to ensure consistency and clarity across classes. Periodic interviews also allow leaders to discern not only the readiness of teachers but their spiritual needs and growth, making instruction a two-way process of edification. Teaching is a spiritual gift, not just an assignment, and those called to it deserve support in magnifying their stewardship. Restoring this infrastructure would affirm the sacredness of teaching the word of God and would help shift the cultural expectation from lesson facilitation to doctrinal exposition, thereby blessing both teachers and learners alike.

Create a Calling or Informal Role: "Scripture Consultant"

To support doctrinal integrity and enrich local instruction, wards and stakes could consider creating a formal or informal role akin to a "Scripture Consultant." This calling would be filled by a doctrinally seasoned member—such as a seminary or institute teacher, a returned missionary with demonstrated scriptural fluency, or someone with academic training in theology or religious education. The primary function of the Scripture Consultant would be to assist teachers and speakers in preparing lessons and talks grounded in the Standard Works, helping them identify relevant passages, frame doctrinal insights, and avoid speculative or doctrinally weak content. This would not replace personal revelation or diminish the individual responsibility to prepare spiritually, but rather act as a resource to elevate instructional quality and confidence. Especially in wards where gospel literacy is uneven, this consultative role could become a quiet anchor, enhancing both doctrinal unity and scriptural depth across meetings. Much like a music director enhances worship through order and training, a Scripture Consultant could help restore a culture in which the word of God is taught clearly and with power (see Alma 17:2–3).

Recommend Interviews Include Scripture-Based Reflection

Temple recommend interviews serve as sacred checkpoints in a member's discipleship, affirming both worthiness and ongoing spiritual devotion. To further root this process in the revealed word of God, interview protocols could include a simple invitation for members to share a recent scripture—verse, story, or teaching—that has deepened their understanding of the gospel or strengthened their testimony of Jesus Christ. This is not intended as a test of memory or doctrinal precision, but as a meaningful indicator of engagement with the scriptures as a living well of spiritual nourishment. Such a practice would gently signal that immersion in the Standard Works is not peripheral, but central to covenantal discipleship. It would also normalize a culture in which scripture becomes part of one's spiritual self-assessment, just as prayer, obedience, and service are. In a time when gospel knowledge risks being replaced by sentiment or superficiality, restoring scripture as a touchstone in the most sacred ecclesiastical interviews would affirm its role as both mirror and compass—helping members "remember, and perish not" (Helaman 5:12).

Encourage Questions and Faithful Wrestling in Classes

A mature scriptural culture demands curiosity, engagement, and the willingness to "wrestle before God" (Enos 1:2). To that end, gospel instruction could normalize open-ended, theologically rich questions that invite discussion, exploration, and faithful reflection. Rather than discouraging complexity or ambiguity, teachers could model how to navigate difficult passages, paradoxes, and evolving understanding with reverence and trust in divine truth. This approach echoes the pattern of the Savior, who often taught through questions and parables that prompted listeners to think deeply and seek personal revelation (e.g., Matthew 16:15; Luke 10:36). Faithful inquiry should not be treated as doubt in disguise, but as a covenantal responsibility—a hallmark of spiritual maturity and scriptural literacy. By cultivating classroom environments where sincere questions are welcomed and addressed with patience, charity, and doctrinal clarity, the Church can rebuild a culture of discipleship grounded not in shallow consensus, but in shared pursuit of truth. Ultimately, a questioning heart—anchored in faith and tethered to the scriptures—becomes fertile ground for revelation, inspiration, and conversion.

Encourage Students to Ask Better Questions of Their Leaders

One of the most vital yet underdeveloped aspects of discipleship is the cultivation of meaningful, courageous questions—especially those directed toward local and general Church leadership. Teachers in the Church could intentionally foster a culture in which students learn not only to receive instruction but to seek deeper understanding through informed and faithful inquiry. This is not about fostering contrarianism, but about nurturing doctrinal discernment, spiritual maturity, and the kind of bold engagement modeled by figures like Joseph Smith, who sought wisdom "by study and also by faith" (D&C 88:118). Leaders are sustained not merely by silent loyalty, but by a membership that asks sincere, thoughtful questions in the pursuit of truth. When members learn to approach leaders with humility, reverence, and scriptural grounding, they contribute to a culture of accountability, dialogue, and growth. Encouraging such questions empowers Saints to move beyond passive consumption and into active discipleship—discerning not only what is taught, but how it aligns with covenantal principles and the revealed word of God. In this way, asking better questions becomes not an act of rebellion, but an expression of spiritual integrity.

Call Out False Doctrine—Lovingly, but Clearly

In a scripturally literate community, false doctrine should not be ignored or passively absorbed, but addressed with clarity, humility, and charity. Teachers and leaders have a sacred responsibility to gently but firmly correct sentiment-based distortions, speculative traditions, and ideologically driven rhetoric when they arise in Church discourse. Whether in the form of feel-good heresies, doctrinal confusion, or partisan interpretations of gospel principles, such teachings can erode foundational truths and lead to confusion or apostasy over time. As Paul taught Timothy, those called to teach must "rightly divide the word of truth" and "in meekness instruct those that oppose themselves" (2 Timothy 2:15, 25). Corrective teaching need not be confrontational, but it must be courageous. When falsehoods are left unchecked—particularly in lessons, testimonies, or public settings—they subtly redefine doctrine and displace scriptural authority. A culture that prizes peace over truth will eventually lose both.

Re-center Family Scripture Study as a Priesthood Duty

In the restored Church, the home is the primary classroom of discipleship. To that end, family scripture study could be reframed not as an optional devotional habit, but as a sacred priesthood duty. Heads of households, particularly fathers holding priesthood keys within the family unit, bear covenantal responsibility to lead their families in the word of God. Bishoprics and ward councils could support this by inquiring regularly—not to induce guilt, but to equip and sustain. Such conversations can offer encouragement, share resources, and identify barriers to consistent engagement. Just as priesthood interviews explore Sabbath observance, tithing, and prayer, so too could they gently reinforce the expectation that families are nourished by the scriptures. Re-centering scripture study as a priesthood duty realigns the spiritual governance of the home with its eternal purpose—to raise up a generation grounded in the covenants, fluent in the word, and prepared to build Zion. When parents prioritize the scriptures at home, the Church becomes a spiritually literate people, fortified from the foundation up.

Create Stricter Guidelines for Fast and Testimony Sundays

Fast and testimony meetings are sacred occasions intended to edify the body of Christ and reaffirm collective faith in the restored gospel. However, without gentle structure, these meetings can sometimes drift from their intended spiritual purpose. To preserve doctrinal focus and reverence, Church leadership could consider implementing a brief, standardized statement—read monthly by a member of the Bishopric— reaffirming the centrality of Jesus Christ, the Restoration, the scriptures, and personal witness of revealed truth. Such a statement would not restrict sincere expressions of faith, but rather orient them toward the foundational tenets of the gospel. This simple liturgical prompt could remind members that testimonies are not personal updates, emotional ramblings, or philosophical musings, but sacred declarations grounded in revealed truth (see Alma 5:45–46). By re-centering testimony on Christ and the scriptures, the Church would reinforce both doctrinal clarity and spiritual reverence, helping to protect fast and testimony meetings from drifting into cultural familiarity and instead anchoring them in covenantal purpose.

Re-teach How to Bear Testimony with Doctrine

Bearing testimony is a sacred act of covenant affirmation, yet in contemporary practice it often drifts into vague emotionalism or generalized "feeling language." While sincerity should never be discouraged, it is vital that testimonies reflect doctrinal substance and scriptural clarity. Members of the Church, particularly youth and new converts, could be explicitly taught how to bear witness in ways that affirm revealed truth, draw upon sacred texts, and center on Jesus Christ and his gospel. Testimonies should not merely declare, "I know the Church is true," but rather affirm covenantal realities—the divinity of the Savior, the restoration of priesthood authority, the Book of Mormon as a sacred witness of the covenant path, and the eternal significance of temple ordinances. Scriptural references can provide anchoring language and theological weight, transforming testimonies from private sentiments into public declarations of enduring truth. Leaders and teachers can model this in word and example, gently guiding the Saints toward a testimony culture marked not only by heartfelt conviction, but by covenantal precision and doctrinal depth. This reorientation would help restore the testimony meeting as a setting of communal edification rooted in the word of God.

Reframe Fifth Sunday

Fifth Sunday meetings represent a unique opportunity within the Church calendar to depart from standard instruction and focus on special themes. Rather than reserving these meetings solely for administrative updates or reactive discussions, stakes and wards could consider reframing Fifth Sunday as a recurring "Scripture Revival Sabbath." These meetings would center on the public reading of sacred texts, doctrinal exposition, and testimonies rooted explicitly in scriptural engagement. Members could be invited in advance to share how specific passages have transformed their understanding of Christ, deepened their covenants, or brought spiritual renewal. Leaders might read aloud from chapters often overlooked or misunderstood, modeling reverent interpretation and faithful application. This liturgical realignment would not only promote scriptural fluency but would also renew reverence for the Standard Works as living oracles for the latter days. In a time when many Saints feel disconnected from the depth of gospel doctrine, a Fifth Sunday consecrated to the scriptures could become a recurring anchor of collective devotion, rekindling spiritual appetite.

Host Quarterly Scripture-Deepening Firesides

To foster a culture of scriptural fluency and theological maturity, wards and stakes could consider instituting quarterly "Scripture-Deepening Firesides." These gatherings would provide a space outside the standard block schedule for exploring complex gospel themes through sustained engagement with the scriptures. Led by seminary and institute teachers, trained scholars, or doctrinally seasoned members, such firesides could model faithful exegesis, introduce historical and literary context, and demonstrate how to trace doctrinal patterns across the Standard Works. Topics might include covenant theology, grace and discipleship, the typology of Christ in the Book of Mormon, or the symbolic structure of temple language. Unlike typical devotionals, these firesides would not aim merely to uplift emotionally, but to equip intellectually and spiritually— providing Saints with tools for deeper study and greater doctrinal discernment. In an age where religious knowledge is often fragmented or sentimentalized, such initiatives would help recover the sacred rigor of scriptural study and invite members to love the Lord with all their "heart, might, mind, and strength" (D&C 4:2; cf. Mark 12:30).

Institute a Scripture Fluency Initiative in Youth Programs

To cultivate a generation rooted in the word of God, the Church could consider implementing a scripture memory or fluency initiative within youth programs. Such an effort would intentionally ground young Latter-day Saints in core doctrinal passages—key scriptures from the Standard Works that articulate covenant theology, the nature of Christ, and essential principles of the plan of salvation. Memorization need not be rote or performative, but should be coupled with contextual teaching and spiritual reflection, enabling youth not only to recite but to internalize and explain sacred texts. As evidenced in both ancient Israelite tradition and early Christian discipleship, the practice of hiding the word in one's heart (Psalm 119:11) serves as a spiritual safeguard and identity-forming discipline. In a world saturated with competing narratives, anchoring youth in the language and logic of scripture is a necessity. A generation that knows the voice of the Lord in his own words will be far better equipped to discern truth, resist deception, and carry forward the mantle of discipleship into an uncertain future.

Reinstate Third Hour and Offer an Optional Fourth Hour

To restore depth and consistency in doctrinal instruction, Church leadership could consider reinstating a third hour of Sunday meetings—particularly to reestablish weekly Gospel Doctrine classes. The shift to a two-hour block has emphasized home-centered learning, but in many wards, this has unintentionally reduced sustained scriptural engagement. Reintroducing a regular Gospel Doctrine hour would provide essential continuity and collective accountability in the study of scripture. In addition, high-engagement wards could offer a voluntary fourth-hour class focused on advanced, verse-by-verse exegetical study. Modeled after seminary or institute formats, this class could benefit members seeking a deeper grasp of covenantal theology, prophetic symbolism, or the historical framework of sacred texts. Such an initiative acknowledges the varying needs of a diverse Church membership, allowing those with hunger for advanced study to be fed without imposing undue burden on all. In an age of increasing scriptural illiteracy, expanding institutional space for sincere scriptural inquiry is prudent.

At its core, this book rests on a single, uncompromising proposition—the Church of Jesus Christ of Latter-day Saints must return to teaching the scriptures.

Not *about* the scriptures.
Not *around* the scriptures.
Not *in light of* the scriptures.
Not abstracted into principles *derived from* the scriptures.

The scriptures themselves—studied, expounded, and internalized in their revealed form. These sacred texts must once again become the living foundation of our instruction, devotion, and discipleship. Without them, the covenant community will quite possibly erode from spiritual malnourishment.

To conclude, I offer what I call *the parable of the two lumberjacks*. Variations of this story have long circulated in leadership and motivational discourse, often illustrating the value of preparation and renewal. It is perhaps most famously echoed in Stephen R. Covey's "sharpen the saw" principle—a reminder that without continual reorientation to our source of strength, even our most fervent effort becomes diminished.

The Parable of the Two Lumberjacks

Deep in a quiet forest, there lived two lumberjacks, each in a small cabin not far from the other. Both were strong, and both loved their work—felling timber from the dense woods that stretched for miles in every direction.

The first lumberjack rose well before dawn each day. By 4:00 a.m., his ax was in hand, and he was already deep in the trees. He did not stop—not to rest, not to eat, not even to drink. He took pride in his pace, pushing through pain and exhaustion with grit and resolve. He cherished the rhythm of chopping, the ache in his arms, the sweat on his brow. At day's end, there were often bloodstains on his axe from worn hands. Each day, he returned home with exactly ten trees felled—each one earned by sheer force of will.

The second lumberjack began each day more slowly. He woke with the sun, ate bread and honey on his porch, and listened to the wind moving through the branches. After this, he would make his way into the woods at a calm, deliberate pace. He worked hard, but stopped each hour to rest, reflect, and eat from his packed lunch. Each day, by early evening, he returned home having felled fifteen trees—without strain, without rush, and without injury.

One evening, the first lumberjack passed by his neighbor's cabin and saw the towering stack of timber. Weary and frustrated, he called out:

"How can this be? I rise earlier, work longer, never stop… And yet you, who pause each hour, somehow fell more than I?"

The second lumberjack smiled and replied gently, "Because, my friend, I pause every hour to sharpen my ax."

Like the weary lumberjack whose blade dulls from relentless effort, many in the Church today find themselves spiritually exhausted—not for lack of faith or activity, but for neglect of the very source of spiritual renewal. Scripture study is not an academic indulgence. It is not optional enrichment. It is covenantal maintenance. It is the sharpening of the blade, without which all other spiritual labor—callings, meetings, ministering, worship—becomes heavy, fruitless, and unsustainable.

To those who feel spiritually famished, disillusioned, or even ashamed of how long it's been since they opened the scriptures—
This is not a rebuke.
It is an invitation.

There is still time.
The blade can be restored.
The strength can return.
You are not alone.

And to those who see things differently—who may disagree with the tone or conclusions offered here—I extend peace. I hold no animosity toward you—only shared concern for the vitality of the gospel in our lives. If we differ in approach, may we yet be united in desire that Christ remain at the center and that his word be planted deep in the soil of our Zion-bound hearts.

"And now, I would commend you to seek this Jesus of whom the prophets and apostles have written."
(*Ether 12:41*)

Afterword

Famine in Zion was written from a place of faith—as a concerned yet committed member of the Church of Jesus Christ of Latter-day Saints. Throughout the book, I have sought to make clear that, even in instances where I believe lapses in judgment may have occurred among general authorities, I extend the assumption of good intent on the part of Church leadership.

Nevertheless, it would be intellectually dishonest to ignore the reality that several recent institutional decisions—such as the shift to a home-centered, Church-supported model; the watered down principle-based curriculum; the reduction to a two-hour Sunday block; and the elimination of scripture memorization requirements in youth programs like seminary—represent *deliberate* moves away from rigorous scriptural engagement.

Scripture itself commands us to "try the spirits" and discern them "by their fruits." In that spirit, one must at least acknowledge that such intentional steps away from scripture-based instruction could reasonably raise suspicion and concern. While it is difficult—and deeply uncomfortable—to consider the possibility that religious leaders might intentionally make decisions detrimental to the spiritual health of their community, history reminds us that such outcomes are not without precedent.

As a critical reflection, I believe it is worthwhile to entertain a theoretical exercise—What might a religious institution gain by fostering scriptural illiteracy among its members? The Book of Mormon repeatedly warns against secret combinations—clandestine factions such as the Gadianton robbers—who infiltrate societies, distort truth, and manipulate power for personal or political gain. Mormon and Moroni's insistence on including these accounts suggests that such warnings were intended for our time.

While I am certainly not suggesting a direct comparison, the pattern of suppressing knowledge for institutional control is a cautionary tale worth considering. If we are to take the scriptural mandate seriously—to search, study, and treasure up the word of God—then it is imperative that we remain vigilant, not just as disciples, but as stewards of the restored gospel in its fullness.

An intentional tapering of a healthy scriptural diet can yield several consequential outcomes for a religious institution. Chief among these is the consolidation of doctrinal control—when scriptural engagement diminishes, few are equipped to recognize or challenge shifts in doctrine. Scriptural illiteracy also tends to reduce dissent, as members lack the theological framework necessary to evaluate or question institutional teachings. In such environments, leadership may more easily conflate sincere prophetic concern with apostasy, thereby insulating itself from critique.

Moreover, diminished scriptural engagement can facilitate broader institutional growth. Simplified messaging, devoid of theological nuance, is more easily exported and embraced across diverse global populations. Paradoxically, then, scriptural illiteracy can serve as an engine for expansion.

Perhaps most significantly, it fosters increased dependency on institutional authority. In the absence of personal scriptural fluency, members may find it easier to follow leaders than to "search the scriptures" for themselves. In each of these dynamics, interpretive power shifts from sacred text to institutional voice. While such a shift may seem functionally harmless, it poses serious risks if that authority becomes compromised by internal apostasy, institutional drift, or the influence of secret combinations.

In the case of the Church of Jesus Christ of Latter-day Saints, I cannot bring myself to seriously consider the aforementioned possibilities without experiencing a profound sense of unease. I continue to sustain both general and local leaders of the Church in faith and sincerity, and I strive to assume their best intentions. However, if I shift the question from what the Church might *gain* from the gradual reduction of doctrinal literacy—beginning in the Correlation era of the 1960s and accelerating in recent decades—to what it might *lose* by restoring such literacy, one answer becomes particularly clear.

A scripturally literate membership is better equipped to study and contextualize the scriptures broadly, including the Doctrine and Covenants, thereby engaging more critically with Church history. The Church has long struggled with transparency in its historical narratives, often sanitizing or omitting troubling episodes. In many cases, members have faced formal membership restrictions (disfellowshipment) or withdrawal of records (excommunication) for allegedly false claims that the Church later acknowledged as true. A recent example includes the February 2025 publication in the Church's digital library of the long-disputed 1886 revelation to President John Taylor, affirming the permanence of the practice of plural marriage—a document that for decades Church leaders publicly denied or dismissed as fraudulent.

While the Church has made strides toward transparency in the internet era—particularly in the past 10 to 15 years—it has still not adequately equipped members to navigate historical and doctrinal complexity. This is largely because teaching nuance often necessitates a degree of institutional humility, including acknowledgment of past errors or misleading representations. Studies and personal accounts repeatedly show that the predominant reason members leave the Church is not sin, apathy, or worldliness, but a deep sense of betrayal—most often related to historical issues and the perceived concealment of truth.

My sincere hope—and belief—is that this remains only a thought experiment, not a reflection of reality. To be clear, I am not suggesting that the Church is intentionally fostering scriptural illiteracy for institutional gain or to prevent institutional loss. However, I am suggesting that tolerating scriptural illiteracy is dangerous precisely because it leaves the door open for such corruption to take root. If that day ever comes, I certainly hope the Church prioritizes the preservation of its integrity over the preservation of its membership.

Note from the Author

I don't lose sleep over many things. I've lost sleep over this.

For quite some time, I've carried a growing concern about the matters addressed in this book. Normally, I keep such thoughts to myself. I had other projects in mind, other responsibilities I expected to be pursuing at this stage. I didn't want this to be a book. In many ways, I still don't. But, as I explain in the preface, the pressure to write this became too strong to ignore. It built steadily over weeks, manifesting with the kind of spiritual discomfort people often describe when resisting a prompting to bear testimony during a fast and testimony meeting.

I began writing on May 11, 2025, and completed the initial draft in the early morning hours of May 18. What occurred during that week was unlike anything I've experienced before. Words flowed through me with an urgency and clarity that I can only describe as inspired. The text poured out at a rate of about 10,000 words per day, which is categorically abnormal for me, and frankly, categorically abnormal in general. When I reached the final page, though there was still editing and refinement ahead, I felt a deep and liberating sense of relief. A burden had been lifted from me.

Now, a different kind of burden presses on me—the feeling that I must share what I have written. At first, I hoped to quietly publish it online, with no marketing, no attention, no public association, and perhaps even under a pseudonym. This is the kind of work that could draw misunderstanding or criticism, and I don't desire either. I'm a private, introverted person. I avoid the spotlight. The idea of sharing this with local or general Church leadership has made me want to shrink back into silence.

But the more I resist the prompting to share it, the more persistent it becomes. I feel a spiritual pull that I cannot ignore. I am now persuaded that I must share this, not only with my bishop and stake president, but with the First Presidency, the Quorum of the Twelve, and the Sunday

School General Presidency. Even writing that sentence makes me squeamish. But I cannot shake the impression that this is what I am supposed to do.

I believe this work could only have been produced under the influence of spiritual inspiration. And if that is true, then I must act accordingly. The words of Christ to Peter echo in my mind—*"When thou art converted, strengthen thy brethren"* (Luke 22:32). To withhold this out of fear or self-consciousness may amount to willful silence in a moment that demands a voice. I have asked myself whether I bear a moral or covenantal responsibility to make this work known, however small my voice may be. I do not wish to run from the Spirit if He is prompting me to speak.

Yes, there is risk in sharing this. But there is greater risk in withholding it. Should this book ever surface more broadly in the future, I would rather be remembered as someone who brought it forward in faith and transparency than be seen as secretly critical or evasive of counsel. Sharing it now, while it is still quiet, allows for honest and constructive engagement within ecclesiastical channels.

Even if my leaders do not agree with all of my conclusions, perhaps this effort could foster better-informed relationships, create space for mutual understanding, or contribute to spiritually accountable dialogue in my ward or stake. I can only hope so.

I wonder if thoughts like these crossed the mind of Samuel the Lamanite as he prepared to climb that wall…

Above all, I want to say that I may be wrong about some of what I've written. I'm open to correction. But I have chosen to speak because I love the Church too deeply to remain silent and simply hope for the best. My hope is not to tear down, but to build—to warn where warning is needed, and to lift wherever I can. This book is offered in that spirit.

— *J.M. Sobczak*
May 25, 2025

Made in the USA
Monee, IL
08 July 2025

20534588R00100